Comfort
&Spice

Comfort & Spice

NIAMH SHIELDS

Quadrille
PUBLISHING

Editorial Director Anne Furniss
Creative Director Helen Lewis
Project Editor Lucy Bannell
Designers Nicola Davidson, Jim Smith
Photographer Georgia Glynn Smith
Production Director Vincent Smith
Production Controller James Finan

First published in 2011 by Quadrille Publishing Limited
Alhambra House, 27–31 Charing Cross Road, London WC2H 0LS
www.quadrille.co.uk

Cataloguing in Publication Data: a catalogue record for this book
is available from the British Library.

ISBN 978 184949 012 2

Printed in China

✦ CONTENTS ✦

I love to eat and I love to cook. It gives me very great pleasure. Food doesn't need to be complicated, nor does it need to be fussy. Recipes can take hours, or they can take minutes, the end result can always be wonderful food.

I love to cook for myself, my family and friends. I love seeing their faces light up when they sample something delicious that I have prepared for them … then I force them to take the recipe home and try it for themselves. My friends' weeks are now littered with instances of my prawn curry and meatballs, among other things, and this makes me very happy. Cooking really isn't tough!

'But you must be a chef? I can't do that.' I'm not! I am an enthusiastic home cook. And, better again, I'm predominantly self-taught, so really you can do it, too. Go to your butcher, buy some brisket and slow cook it. Get some squid from your fishmonger – and ask him to prepare it, too – for a week night supper. Embrace life and embrace your kitchen. We would all be so much better for it if we did!

I adore spices and flavour, comfort and fun, food that zings and sizzles. Quick week day recipes and long weekend ones, where my oven does the work while I drink some wine, or often while I sleep.

Simple inexpensive food comes to life with a little bit of attention from some appropriate fresh spices. 'Oh, but I hate spicy food.' I promise you, you don't. Spices don't always mean heat, they mean flavour. Treat your spice box as a paint palette and watch your food come to life. With a £10 investment in fresh spices every six months, you can change the way you eat and the way you cook.

Slow cooking makes tough meat supple, yielding and far more delicious than those more expensive cuts. Leftovers from the weekends make week day evenings quick, simple and a joy.

So this book is for all of you who are maybe afraid to cook. It's also for those of you who love spending time in your kitchen and are interested in learning about different ways of cooking and expanding your repertoire. I hope you like it.

How to be a better cook

So, you love to cook but want to be better. What should you do?

Shop clever

Choose your produce well. The best food comes from the very best ingredients. Poor ingredients will produce a poor result, even when the very best chef is cooking them.

Always use free-range eggs; organic if possible. I use large free-range organic eggs, which have larger, more flavourful egg yolks. The flavour is far superior, they cook better and are not full of chemical rubbish as the chickens haven't been pumped with antibiotics or other chemicals.

Always use unwaxed lemons; you wouldn't shave a candle into your dinner now would you? They have much better flavour too.

Eat seasonally, when ingredients are at their best and much cheaper.

Buy from independent retailers. They are often cheaper, the produce is almost always better, they know their product very well and can give you great advice on what to do with it.

In the kitchen

Teach yourself the basics, those building blocks will make a huge difference both to your cooking and to your confidence.

Make homemade stock, it takes time not energy and is a great use of those vegetables that are lingering in your fridge.

Trust your nose and palate and learn to understand balance in food. If it needs to be sweeter, add some sugar or honey; sour, add some vinegar, tamarind or sumac; salty, add some salt!

Don't be afraid of fat and salt. In moderation they are fine and they taste good, too.

Big flavours

Add flavour where you can, it makes a big difference. The gentle aroma of a bay leaf can change a soup, some simple spices can make a roast.

Use sea salt and freshly ground pepper. They will enhance your dish.

Play around with salt, it's fun and it makes your cooking interesting! Salt goes with everything. Two of my favourites are ham salt and rosemary salt. They are fun, different and packed with flavour.

This is so good on eggs or sprinkled on asparagus. Subtle but absolutely delicious, it beats truffle salt hands down any day and is so much cheaper. It's easy too.

Ham salt

Makes about 175g
6 slices Parma ham or jamón Serrano, as thin as possible
150g sea salt

Preheat your oven to 150°C/300°F/gas mark 2.

Place your ham slices on some greaseproof paper and cook gently until completely crisp but not burned; this will take about 15 minutes. Don't use any oil, they need to be as dry as possible.

Allow to cool on a wire tray and, when cold, crumble between your fingers until like a powder.

Mix with the sea salt and store in your fridge.

This is lovely with lamb or pork and is a quick and easy way of jazzing up a simple piece of meat. It's great with white beans, too.

Rosemary salt

Makes about 160g
5 sprigs of rosemary
150g sea salt

Chop the rosemary needles as finely as you can and mix in with the salt. Store in the fridge.

Experiment
Play and enjoy. You won't regret it. You will learn a lot, too.

Most importantly, have fun and don't forget to enjoy eating the fruits of your labours.

Brunch

Cosy weekend brunches for two

I love brunch. It is my favourite and most perfect meal of the week. After rushing around from Monday to Friday, grabbing a bite of breakfast as I head for the door, it's a weekend luxury. Feet up with a big pot of coffee, the papers, sparkling water and juice. You should eat it in your PJs to make the picture complete. None of these recipes will demand too much of you, but they will all taste great.

There are many reasons to make homemade yogurt. It's simple, it's natural, it's cheap and it tastes better. You just need a starter (natural yogurt) and some milk (to convert to yogurt) and some time. The end result is yogurt that is sweeter and nicer than any you can buy. Ideally you let it ferment in a Thermos flask, although at room temperature is fine, too (it just may take a little longer). I like to use Jersey or Guernsey milk for this as the richer the milk, the better the flavour. I love it for a quick breakfast or brunch with a simple fruit compote. Use honey or sugar, whichever you prefer.

Homemade yogurt with rhubarb compote

Serves 6 (but obviously you can keep some for later in the week!)
For the yogurt
1 litre full-fat milk
50g natural yogurt

For the rhubarb compote
400g rhubarb
up to 75g brown sugar (depending on how tart your rhubarb is)
juice of 1 orange

The night before, bring the milk to a simmer and turn off the heat. Let the temperature drop to 40°C/104°F. You can check the temperature with a thermometer, or just put your finger in: if it's just that little bit too hot, then you're there.

Add the yogurt and stir. Seal in a Thermos, or covered and at room temperature, for seven or eight hours. When the yogurt is ready, the milk will have thickened and formed lumps. This is fine and what you expect. Whisk thoroughly and refrigerate to prevent it culturing further and becoming too sour.

For your compote, put the rhubarb, sugar, orange juice and 1 tbsp water into a pan and bring to a boil. Reduce the heat and cook for five minutes, until the rhubarb comes apart at the touch of a fork. Stir, let cool and store in the fridge in an airtight jar. Serve on top of your lovely homemade yogurt.

Homemade porridge, made using good natural oats (not the quick oats that you can get now), is a perfect start to the day. Using full-fat milk it is rich and creamy, not the insipid, thick mass most of us associate with our childhood. It is even better if you soak the oats the night before. Apple and cinnamon is a lovely combination, especially with a little honey to sweeten. With regard to the oats, my preference is Irish … but that shouldn't surprise you very much!

Apple and cinnamon porridge

Serves 1
50g porridge oats
250ml full-fat milk
1 Bramley apple, peeled and chopped into small dice
1 cinnamon stick
honey, to serve

Put the oats into a bowl and stir in the milk. Cover and leave in the fridge overnight.

In the morning, tip the oats and milk into a saucepan. Bring to just before a boil with the apple and cinnamon stick, then reduce the heat to low and cook gently, stirring occasionally to ensure that the porridge doesn't stick, for 10 minutes.

When the apple is cooked and the porridge is lovely and soft, add honey to taste and eat while hot.

The beginning of the asparagus season is one of the most exciting times of the year for me. It is a glorious vegetable, whether you are using the small frail sprue or thick sturdy stalks. Very fresh asparagus is best and sweetest, as the sugars in this vegetable break down into starch quite quickly. For this recipe, use stalks that are reasonably thick and will stay sturdy and tall. The simplicity and quickness of this is its secret. You want the asparagus to retain some crispness, and the egg yolks to be perfectly soft. Asparagus loves eggs, ham loves eggs, asparagus loves ham... this is one of those love-in dishes, where each bite will be delicious, and you will mourn each one.

This may seem like a small detail, but do ensure your eggs are at room temperature before you cook them or they will likely crack. In fact I always keep them at room temperature. They don't need to be kept chilled and egg shells are porous and will absorb other flavours in the fridge. They keep perfectly well in a dark cupboard at room temperature. You won't need to salt your eggs as the ham is already quite salty.

Asparagus and ham soldiers with eggs

Serves 2
12 asparagus spears
12 slices cured ham (Parma, jamón or similar)
4 eggs

Trim the woody ends of the asparagus spears (bend them until they snap naturally in the right place).

Blanch the asparagus spears in boiling water for two minutes, until starting to soften. Run under cold water until the asparagus is cold and has therefore stopped cooking. Dry the asparagus well and wrap each spear in a slice of ham.

Soft-boil each egg in simmering water for four minutes. Meanwhile, griddle or fry each asparagus spear until the ham crisps on either side.

Slice the tops from the eggs and dip the crispy spears into the yolk. And repeat. Delicious!

✦ PASSION ✦

Lemon and ricotta pancakes with raspberries

These fluffy, sweet pancakes are a delight. They are super-easy to make and extra special if you use Homemade Ricotta (see page 70). It may seem a chore to separate eggs, but it makes a very big difference, I promise. If you have a mixer this recipe is really quick, but it's not too taxing by hand either. Think of the pancakes at the end! If raspberries are out of season, substitute with another fruit. The consistency of these pancakes will depend on how much water is in your ricotta, so drain it for half an hour if you can (homemade is best, as always). For perfectly round pancakes you may want to use a mould, but I make mine freeform and sloppy... they still taste great.

Serves 2 (3 pancakes each)
3 eggs, separated
25g unsalted butter, melted
50g caster sugar
finely grated zest of 1 unwaxed lemon, and juice of ½
250g ricotta cheese (homemade is best, see page 70)
pinch of sea salt
110g plain flour, sifted
½ tsp baking powder
light flavourless oil, such as sunflower, to fry
100g raspberries
honey, to serve

Whisk the egg yolks, butter, sugar and lemon zest until fluffy. Whisk in the ricotta, lemon juice, salt, flour and baking powder.

Separately, whisk the egg whites until they start to form peaks. Gently fold them into the batter, taking care not to knock out the air (the air is the fluffiness).

Heat a little oil in a frying pan placed over a medium-high heat. Pour one-sixth of the batter into the hot pan and, when bubbles start appearing, flip. Cook for about two to three minutes longer. Remove from the pan and keep warm while you cook the rest.

Serve in stacks with the raspberries and honey.

The Antipodeans are responsible for me loving this recipe … I have many Antipodean friends in London and frequently visit Antipodean cafes as they have some of the best coffee. It is here that I discovered Bircher muesli. A healthy, flavoursome joy it is, too. (Though I should add that the original was developed many years ago by a Swiss doctor, Maximilian Oskar Bircher-Benner!) It's basically oats soaked in water or milk, with grated apple and other fruits and nuts. This is perfect for me as I can't bear raisins and especially hate them in my morning muesli. This is a great alternative. Extra chopped fruit is a delicious and healthy addition.

Bircher muesli

Serves 2
50g rolled oats
150ml full-fat milk
1 large tart dessert apple (Granny Smith or similar), grated
75g yogurt (homemade is best, see page 12)
honey, to taste
seasonal chopped fruit (optional)
2 tbsp coarsely chopped nuts (I like hazelnuts or almonds)

Soak the oats in the milk for a minimum of 10 minutes, but ideally overnight, covered, in the fridge.
    Add the apple and yogurt and stir through. Add honey to taste.
Serve in bowls with the seasonal fruit, if using, and the nuts on top.

I first made these really simple potato pancakes when in school. It's a traditional Irish dish and a great use of leftover potatoes. It is not to be confused with boxty, another Irish potato cake, which contains grated raw potato. Smoked salmon is a wonderful breakfast fish, especially when it's a good one. My favourite comes from East Cork, where artisan smoker Frank Hederman produces the most wonderful fish smoked over beech wood. Cucumber pickle is a perfect side dish, with just a touch of sugar.

Smoked salmon with potato pancakes and cucumber relish

Serves 2

For the cucumber relish
240ml cider vinegar
200g caster sugar
1 tsp salt
2 cucumbers, sliced as finely as you can

For the pancakes
25g unsalted butter, melted, plus more to fry
30g plain flour, sifted, plus more to dust
2 spring onions, shredded

450g warm mashed potatoes
  (with no butter or milk added)
sea salt
freshly ground black pepper
1 egg
1 tsp light oil, such as sunflower

For the smoked salmon
200g smoked salmon, thinly sliced

For the relish, heat the vinegar, sugar and salt just until the sugar and salt are dissolved. Allow to cool. Pour over the cucumbers and leave overnight in the fridge (or for at least five hours).

To make the pancakes, add the melted butter, flour and spring onions to the mashed potato with a pinch of salt and pepper to taste. Stir with a wooden spoon, adding the egg until it forms a dough.

Knead lightly on a floured work surface, then roll until about 5mm thick. Traditionally, the dough is rolled into a circle and cut into triangles, but you can cut it into circles with a scone cutter or the top of a glass if you prefer.

Fry the pancakes in the oil and a little more butter on a medium heat for a couple of minutes on each side, until brown.

Serve with the smoked salmon and cucumber relish.

Homemade butter

Homemade butter is a joy to make, even better to eat and so very easy. Why bother? Because you can choose the best cream and make any butter you like. I love rich yellow creams such as Jersey or Guernsey that give a beautiful, intense and creamy butter. Use the best cream you can get. You can keep it unsalted (but use it quickly!), or be creative. Make it with sea salt or, for an extra oomph, with smoked or flavoured sea salt. Your friends will be really impressed, I promise! You can even get them to make it.

You can make it simply by putting the cream in a jar and shaking it like crazy until the milk separates from the butter or, my preference, just stick it in a mixer and whip it. The first pass will still be quite milky and, if you leave it like this, it will sour pretty quickly, so squeeze and drain it to get the excess moisture out.

Makes about 300g
350ml double cream, preferably Jersey cream

Whisk the double cream in a mixer, by hand or in a jar until the buttermilk separates from the butter fat. Squeeze the solids with your hands to remove excess liquid and whisk or shake it again. Wrap in muslin or cheesecloth and hang it over the kitchen sink from your tap for an hour or so. Use immediately, or store in the fridge.

Rose petal butter

This butter is beautiful and fragrant, creamy and sweet, a pretty and delicious start to a weekend or special morning. I love it with pancakes or scones.

Makes 250g
250g butter (homemade is best, see above)
petals from 1 organic rose, colour of your choice

With the butter at room temperature, cream it until nice and soft, then gently stir in the rose petals until there are swirls of them throughout. Use immediately or wrap and store in the fridge for a few days.

These fluffy pancakes will make you smile. The crisp, salty bacon with the sweet, soft, bouncy pancakes is a wondrous combination. The maple syrup is that added extra, the bit that almost pushes the dish too far, but makes it perfect. And delicious.

American-style pancakes with bacon and maple syrup

Serves 1; multiply as required
100g plain flour
1 heaped tsp baking powder
1 egg, separated
generous pinch of sea salt
1 tsp brown sugar
100ml full-fat milk
bacon. Streaky for me, but whatever you
    prefer, and as much as you want to eat.
    Three slices for one is a good start!
unsalted butter, to fry
maple syrup, to serve

Sift the flour and baking powder. This is important as the sifting introduces air and will make your pancakes fluffy instead of leaden. Whisk the egg white until it stiffens and forms soft peaks.

Add the salt and sugar to the flour mixture and create a well in the middle. Pour in the egg yolk and the milk. Stir until you get a batter which has no lumps. Fold in the egg white gently, taking care not to knock out the air you've introduced.

Grill the bacon and keep it in a warm oven while you get on with cooking the pancakes.

Heat a frying pan over a medium-high heat. Melt a knob of butter and add a ladleful of pancake mixture. Drop from a few inches above and it will spread to form a circular pancake, or close enough to one.

The pancakes will cook quite quickly. As soon as you see bubbles in the batter they are ready to flip. They cook quickly on the other side too and will need just a minute or so. Take a peek; if browned, they're done.

Keep warm in the oven with the bacon while you cook the rest of the pancakes, adding each pancake to the oven as they cook.

To serve, stack the pancakes with bacon in between and on top. Drizzle the maple syrup over to taste. And you're done.

I love this dish, a cheeky take on Mexican huevos rancheros (eggs on tortillas with spicy salsa). In this I substitute potatoes (of course!), resulting in a super-low effort and tasty dish. Good canned tomatoes are great quality and, outside of tomato season, are better than the fresh tomatoes in the shops, so don't feel bad about using them; you will get the best results. Try San Marzano tomatoes or lovely canned pomodorini. They can be expensive, but they are worth it. The only thing to remember is that they are often a little acidic, so some sugar is best added to counter that.

Brunch baked eggs, aka Irish huevos rancheros

Serves 2
1 red onion, finely chopped
1 tbsp light oil, plus more for the tin
2 garlic cloves, finely chopped
1 red chilli, finely chopped
    (deseeded if you don't like things too hot)
400g can good-quality tomatoes
1 tsp caster sugar
sea salt
freshly ground black pepper
250g potatoes (leftover or boiled until tender),
    in chunks
handful of coriander leaves, chopped
4 eggs

Preheat the oven to 180°C/350°F/gas mark 4.

Make a quick tomato sauce by sautéing the onion in the oil for five minutes over a medium heat until translucent but not brown. Add the garlic and chilli for 30 seconds, then add the tomatoes and sugar. Cook for 15 minutes and season to taste.

Put the potatoes into a lightly oiled roasting tin, add the sauce, and roast for 10 minutes. Sprinkle half the coriander on top and make four spaces for the eggs.

Crack the eggs in and cook for up to five minutes until the whites are set. The yolks will be starting to set too, but should be still soft. Serve with the rest of the coriander sprinkled on top.

The perfect breakfast bread: quick, fluffy and delicious, with the minimum of work. No proving is required and they're ready in five minutes.

Irish soda farls

Serves 2
225g plain flour, plus more to dust
½ tsp salt
1 tsp bicarbonate of soda
150ml buttermilk

Sift the flour, salt and bicarb into a bowl. Create a well in the centre and add the buttermilk gradually, until the dough holds together but is not too wet. Knead briefly (half a minute or so, no more) on a lightly floured surface. Shape into a circle about 1cm thick. Divide into eight wedges.

Heat a frying pan, add a little flour and cook the farls on each side over a medium heat for eight minutes, turning, until golden brown.

Hash was brought to Boston by the Irish on the famine ships. Leftover potatoes are best, they taste much better fried the next day. I don't know why. I make many types of hash with what I have available, but this is a favourite. Poach or fry the eggs; it's up to you.

Chorizo, potato and egg hash

Serves 1
200g leftover boiled potatoes, chopped into 1cm dice
1 tsp light oil, such as sunflower or light olive oil
2 cooking chorizo sausages, chopped into 1cm rounds
1 piquillo pepper, or 1 red pepper, diced
2 eggs
handful of flat leaf parsley, chopped

Sauté the potatoes in a large frying pan over a medium heat in the oil, stirring to make sure they brown all over. Set aside. In the same pan, sauté the chorizo and pepper for five minutes, until the chorizo starts to crisp and the pepper is soft. If you are poaching eggs, do so now. Return the potatoes to the pan and stir in the parsley.

Create some space for the eggs if you are frying them, and crack them in. Cook until the white is set but the yolk is still runny. Eat hot.

I adore black pudding, especially Irish black pudding which is often wholesome with oats and warm with gentle spicing. I like to roast it until it almost bursts and eat it with runny eggs. I also like croquettes, which are so crispy and delicious they are impossible to resist. Use fresh breadcrumbs or Japanese panko. I use panko as I love the texture and they are so convenient. The croquettes are best fried, but you can bake them too. Tomato goes brilliantly with earthy, rich black pudding; the fruity sweetness lightens the intensity. Use the best tomatoes you can get, small tomatoes on the vine roasted until almost bursting with a drizzle of olive oil and a sprinkle of sea salt are perfect.

Black pudding croquettes and roast tomatoes with poached eggs

Serves 1
2 branches of small tomatoes on the vine
    (about 8 tomatoes to a branch)
extra virgin olive oil
sea salt
freshly ground black pepper
2 eggs

For the croquettes
100g plain flour
1 egg
100g breadcrumbs, or panko crumbs
300g black pudding, in 2.5cm chunks
light oil (groundnut or sunflower), to deep-fry

Preheat the oven to 180°C/350°F/gas mark 4. Put the tomatoes in a roasting tin, drizzle with oil, sprinkle with salt and roast for 10 minutes.

Meanwhile, arrange on your work surface three shallow bowls. Put the flour in the first bowl and season it well. Beat the egg in the second bowl. Tip the breadcrumbs into the third. Coat the black pudding first in the flour, then the egg, then the breadcrumbs.

It is best to fry for flavour and texture, either in a deep-fryer, or fill a deep pan with 5cm of oil. Place over a medium-high heat. When a piece of bread fizzes and crisps in the oil immediately, it is ready. Fry the croquettes until brown and crispy. Drain on kitchen paper.

While the croquettes are frying, prepare your eggs (either poached or fried). And you're done. Enjoy your lovely brunch.

Home-baked beans are another simple luxury. I cook up a huge pan of beans and freeze them in 300g batches (the equivalent, roughly, of a can of beans) so I can knock up great bean dishes super-quickly. They really are superior in taste and texture. I find canned beans can be soggy and tasteless. This is worth the effort as it's fresh and spritely and will liven up your breakfast. It keeps well for a few days in the fridge, too. It has a tomato base, some chilli and some summer courgette to give it a spring in its step. You can knock it up in 30 minutes on a summer weekend morning

Home-baked beans with courgette and chilli

Serves 2
1 red onion, finely chopped
1 tbsp olive oil
2 courgettes, quartered lengthways and chopped
2 garlic cloves, finely chopped
1 red chilli, finely chopped (deseeded if you don't like too much heat)
300g cooked haricot, cannellini or other white beans (home-cooked
   are best, see page 160), or 400g can white beans, drained and rinsed
250ml light vegetable or chicken stock
400g can tomatoes
1 tsp caster sugar
1 tbsp balsamic vinegar
sea salt
freshly ground black pepper
handful of basil leaves

Sauté the onion in the olive oil over a medium heat for five minutes, until translucent. Add the courgettes for three minutes or so, until they start to lose some of their water. Add the garlic and chilli for 30 seconds, then add the beans, stock, tomatoes, sugar and balsamic vinegar.
   Cook for 10 minutes and season to taste. Shred the basil and stir through just before serving.

I live a mile from one of the most Turkish streets in London, so I am no stranger to these eggs. They are so simple and surprisingly delicious. The first time I saw them, I knew I just had to try: yogurt, spiced melted butter and poached eggs. Whatever would that taste like? Great!

Don't be afraid of poached eggs, there is no secret. Well, if there is it is simply that your eggs need to be as fresh as possible. A fresh egg has a tight white and it will pull around the yolk when you poach it. Eggs in the shop are usually already a week old, so buy them on the day, or better still in the farmers' market, if you can. I do the whirlpool technique which I was taught. It may seem excessive, but I love a good poached egg. If I am making more than one, I chill the poached eggs in iced water ready to reheat in hot water for 30 seconds when they are all ready. Some people add vinegar, which helps keep the white tight, but if the eggs are fresh this isn't necessary. Whatever works for you. There is a lot of butter in this; do feel free to scale back. You won't regret it if you don't, though. There are three ways of flavouring these: you can go with spice (paprika); or with aroma (sage); or you can even combine the two. The crispy sage leaves are heavenly in the melted butter; the paprika is wonderful too. Try either and try them together as well. I can never decide which I prefer.

Turkish eggs

Serves 1
2 eggs
25g unsalted butter
6 sage leaves, or ½ tsp hot paprika, or both
100g thick Greek yogurt

Poach the eggs. Bring a deep pan of water to a gentle simmer (small bubbles will be rising to the surface, just before a boil).

This is easier to do if you crack each egg into a ramekin or cup so that you can easily drop it into the whirlpool while it's still busy spinning.

Create a little whirlpool by running a spoon around the edges of the simmering water until there is a fast-moving swirl in the centre. Drop in your egg and, when the white is firm, it's done. Repeat with the second egg.

While the eggs are poaching, melt the butter. Crisp the sage leaves in the butter, if using, or add the paprika to the melted butter, if using.

Create a pillow of the yogurt in the bottom of a bowl. Put the poached eggs on top and drizzle that lovely melted butter over them. Add the sage leaves too, if using. The crispy leaves make a wonderful contrast to the creamy, rich egg yolk.

Speedy Suppers

Full-flavoured quick food for week nights

Lots of people tell me that they can't eat well during the week as they are too busy and don't have time. I disagree. There is always half an hour that can be clawed back and dragged to the kitchen for the sake of a quick, delicious, nutritious meal. Some of these dishes take longer than that to cook, but the prep is quick for most, which means that while they are cooking you can go about your normal everyday busy business. Reclaim your evening suppers!

Halloumi is a great Mediterranean cheese easily found now in most supermarkets and in Greek or Turkish shops. It doesn't melt well and so is ideal for frying. It's a perfect thing to serve to vegetarian friends. Very salty, it is lovely in this salad, offset with fruity tomatoes and pomegranate seeds. I add onion for texture and parsley gives it a lift. The dressing is simple and fruity, just pomegranate molasses and olive oil with a tiny bit of red wine vinegar. Some pomegranate molasses can be quite sour and, if yours is, you may not need the vinegar, so taste it before using. It's a killer ingredient. As a dressing or marinade it's a best friend to lamb and chicken as well. I had to refrain from using it in too many recipes in this book!

Halloumi and pomegranate salad

Serves 2
2 tbsp pomegranate molasses
2 tbsp extra virgin olive oil
1 tbsp red wine vinegar
sea salt
freshly ground black pepper
½ red onion, thinly sliced
12 cherry tomatoes, halved
250g block halloumi, cut into 5mm slices
1 tsp light olive oil
seeds of ½ pomegranate
handful of flat leaf parsley, chopped

Make the dressing by combining the pomegranate molasses, extra virgin olive oil and vinegar and stirring thoroughly. Season to taste.

Arrange the red onion slices and tomatoes on two plates.

Lightly fry the halloumi – ideally in a griddle pan to get those lovely dark stripes – in the light olive oil on both sides, for a minute or so each, until brown. Place on top of the onion and tomatoes.

Drizzle with the dressing and scatter with the pomegranate seeds and parsley. Eat at once.

This is a great quick meal but, better still, the leftovers make a great lunchbox. If you're not a fan of chickpeas, feel free to substitute with cooked white beans. Fresh spices, as I reiterate so often in this book, make all the difference. Roasting and grinding your own spices only takes seconds and I strongly recommend you do it. I find sharp feta cheese goes well with gentle, soothing spinach and spicy beans. Serve with toasted pitta bread.

Spiced chickpea, spinach and feta salad

Serves 2
1 tsp coriander seeds
1 tsp cumin seeds
½ tsp turmeric
½ tsp chilli powder
½ tsp garam masala
1 small onion, finely chopped
1 celery stick, finely sliced
1 tbsp light oil, such as sunflower or groundnut
2.5cm fresh root ginger, grated
1 fat garlic clove, finely chopped
100g cherry or baby plum tomatoes, quartered
300g cooked chickpeas (home-cooked are best, see page 160),
    or 400g can chickpeas, drained and rinsed
couple of handfuls of spinach
handful of coriander leaves, chopped
200g feta cheese, crumbled
sea salt
freshly ground black pepper
juice of ½ unwaxed lemon

Toast the coriander and cumin seeds in a dry frying pan until they start to pop; usually no more than one minute. Grind the toasted seeds in a mortar and pestle. Combine with the turmeric, chilli and garam masala.

Fry the onion and celery in the oil until the onion is translucent, then add the spices, ginger and garlic and fry for a minute or so. Add the tomatoes and cook for a couple of minutes.

Add the chickpeas and coat in the spices. Add the spinach and stir until wilted. Take off the heat and stir in the coriander and feta. Season and add lemon juice to taste. The lemon juice lifts the flavours and gives a lovely freshness.

I came across the idea for this recipe when investigating Chinese New Year recipes. These are called 'long life noodles' in China. I love eating for an occasion, even when it is not culturally my own! The idea is that you don't cut or break the noodles as it is very bad luck for your own lifespan. (Although I am sure you'll be OK if you do.)

Tofu is a much underrated ingredient; it carries the flavours of whatever you put with it and is solid protein. It is particularly good with the tannic green tea and sweet red pepper here. Asian – and particularly Japanese – food shops serve terrific fresh tofu, so do investigate there if you can. Most supermarkets do now, too. Go for the packets in the fridge over those on the shelf.

This dish eats really well hot or cold. Leftovers are very good for lunch the next day.

Chinese noodles with tofu and green tea

Serves 2
200g medium egg or udon noodles
2 tbsp light oil, such as sunflower or groundnut
1 tsp green tea leaves, preferably gunpowder
2.5cm fresh root ginger, finely chopped
2 garlic cloves, finely chopped
1 large red pepper, cut into thin strips
200g firm tofu, cut into matchsticks
4 spring onions, cut diagonally into 2.5cm pieces
2 tbsp soy sauce
2 tbsp rice vinegar
1 tsp toasted sesame oil
sea salt
freshly ground black pepper

Bring a large pot of water to a boil. Cook the noodles according to the packet instructions. Drain and rinse with cold water to stop them cooking. Set aside.

Heat the oil in a frying pan or wok over a medium heat. Add the tea leaves, ginger and garlic and cook for about 30 seconds. Add the red pepper and tofu, stirring gently until the peppers begin to soften. Add the noodles and cook for a couple of minutes, stirring gently until the noodles are warmed through.

Add spring onions, soy sauce, rice vinegar and sesame oil. Season to taste and serve.

Lentil soup, harissa croutons

A gentle, smooth red lentil soup is a perfect carrier for spicy, crisp harissa croutons. I love playing with croutons. They are receptive to so many flavours. These harissa croutons are great – spicy and crispy – though a mellow crouton of good bread tossed in Parmesan, parsley and olive oil is terrific in salad. There's so much scope.

Serves 4

1 tbsp harissa (homemade is best, see below)
3 tbsp extra virgin olive oil
sea salt
freshly ground black pepper
100g leftover good bread, cubed
1 tbsp cumin seeds
1 banana shallot, finely chopped
1 tbsp light oil, such as sunflower
1 mild green chilli, finely chopped
1 garlic clove, finely chopped
1.25 litres light vegetable or chicken stock
100g red lentils
200g baby spinach
squeeze of lemon

Preheat the oven to 150°C/300°F/gas mark 2. Combine the harissa and olive oil and season. Toss with the bread to coat. Bake for 20–25 minutes until crisp, shaking occasionally. Meanwhile, place the cumin seeds in a small dry frying pan over a medium heat and stir until aromatic. Grind to a powder in a mortar and pestle.

Sauté the shallot in the oil over a medium heat for five minutes, until translucent. Add the cumin, chilli and garlic and cook for 30 seconds. Pour in the stock and lentils; cook for 10–15 minutes until the lentils break down. Pack in the spinach, stir to wilt and turn off the heat. Squeeze over lemon, season and serve with the spicy croutons.

Tip: to make **homemade harissa**, roast a red pepper over a gas flame until black all over. Place in a plastic bag and allow to cool. Blitz with 4 red chillies, deseeded, 1 tbsp toasted and ground cumin seeds, 2 garlic cloves, chopped, 1 tsp red wine vinegar and 2 tbsp extra virgin olive oil and season with sea salt.

This is a heady combination of deep savoury flavours, very rich and moreish. Called *nasu dengaku* in Japan, it is perfect comfort food. It will sooth any tender tum and take you right away from anything that is bothering you when you first bite into it.

I first had this dish on a trip to Japan and subsequently many times in Japanese restaurants in London. Luckily, it is super-easy to make at home, too. A simple trinity of mirin (rice wine), sake and miso dominate, with sugar to sweeten, savoury sesame oil and seeds. It's perfect with plain white rice, with which you will chase the remaining miso around the plate.

The ingredients are very easy to source; most large supermarkets will have all of these things. There are many types of miso paste, a sweet white variety is best but all will do well. Don't be tempted to substitute packets of miso soup, it won't be very nice! Use good miso for the best results.

Aubergine with miso

Serves 2
1 tbsp mirin, or light sherry
1 tbsp sake
1 tbsp caster sugar
3 tbsp miso paste
1 large aubergine, halved lengthways
1 tbsp light oil, such as groundnut
1 tbsp sesame seeds

Make the sauce by heating the mirin, sake and sugar and boiling the alcohol off over a couple of minutes. Reduce the heat and add the miso. Cook gently for a few more minutes.

Slash the aubergine diagonally through the flesh at 2.5cm intervals. Put cut side down into a frying pan with the oil over a medium heat. Cook on this side for two minutes.

Turn over and cook on the skin side until the aubergine is soft to the touch and a knife goes easily through it. It should take a maximum of five minutes, but will depend on the size of your aubergine.

Heat the grill and spoon the sauce over each aubergine half. Sprinkle with the sesame seeds and grill until the sauce is bubbling.

Serve immediately with rice.

Tip: the little aubergines that you find in Asian food shops – and increasingly in supermarkets – cooked this way make terrific grazing food for friends.

Any white fish or salmon works really well in fish cakes, but it's hard to beat a good smoked haddock. These are quick and filling, leftovers make great lunch and, if you want to make extra for another night, they freeze really well.

Smoked haddock fish cakes with green salad

Serves 4
For the fish cakes
1 onion
10 cloves
1 litre full-fat milk
3 bay leaves
400g smoked haddock (preferably undyed)
900g potatoes
handful of flat leaf parsley, roughly chopped
50g unsalted butter (optional), plus more to fry
3 spring onions, finely sliced
sea salt
freshly ground black pepper

2 eggs, beaten
100g plain flour
200g breadcrumbs
olive oil, to fry

For the salad
1 head green lettuce of your choice, separated into leaves
12 cherry tomatoes, halved
2 spring onions, finely chopped
juice of ½ unwaxed lemon
2 tbsp extra virgin olive oil

Halve the onion, peel and stud with the cloves. Add to the milk and bay leaves in a pan that can take the fish lying flat. Bring to just below a simmer, reduce the heat and add the haddock, ensuring it is covered with milk. Leave to poach gently for 15 minutes or so, ensuring the milk never boils. Allow the fish to cool and flake gently.

Boil the potatoes until tender, then mash. Add the fish to the mash with the parsley, butter, if using, spring onions and some of the poaching milk, if required (only if your mash is dry; you don't want it sloppy though). Season with salt and pepper. Shape into eight large or 12 smaller balls and flatten until they are no more than 2cm thick.

Place the eggs in a shallow bowl, and the flour in a second, seasoning the flour well. Put the breadcrumbs on a plate. Coat each fish cake in flour, then in egg, then breadcrumbs. If you want more breadcrumbs on the cakes, repeat the egg and crumb layers again.

Make your salad by combining all the ingredients and dressing with the lemon and extra virgin olive oil, seasoning to taste.

Shallow-fry the fish cakes in a mixture of olive oil and butter over a medium heat for about five minutes on each side, taking care they don't burn. Serve warm with the salad.

This is a great way of livening up some salmon, adding a crunchy texture and making it healthier, too. Sesame seeds are super-healthy and have been shown to have a cholesterol-lowering effect. Could this dish be any healthier? I don't think it could. My favourite almonds are Spanish Marcona: small, round and delicious, they have a gorgeous flavour and are a good size. Any almonds will do however. They make a lovely textural contrast with the juicy tomatoes and this salad to me screams health. Enjoy it and use it to balance out one of your pork days, that's what I do! The quality of the ingredients is important here; a poor balsamic vinegar won't be jammy enough to liven up the tomatoes, while bad tomatoes just taste bad, so get the best you can and enjoy.

Sesame-crusted salmon with tomato and almond salad

Serves 2
For the salmon
50g sesame seeds
2 x 150g salmon fillets
2 tbsp olive oil
1 tbsp light oil

For the salad
75g almonds, preferably Marcona
200g good tomatoes, in 1cm dice
75g rocket leaves
1 tbsp good balsamic vinegar
2 tbsp extra virgin olive oil
sea salt
freshly ground black pepper

Place the sesame seeds in a shallow bowl or on a plate. Coat the salmon in the olive oil and then in the seeds, coating all sides.

Fry the salmon in the light oil over a medium heat for six to eight minutes, turning once, until cooked through but still very tender in the middle. Take care not to burn the seeds or overcook the fish.

Meanwhile, toast the almonds quickly in a dry pan. Gently combine with the tomatoes and rocket, then dress with the balsamic and oil. Season to taste.

Serve the fish hot on top of the salad.

I love this recipe and it is one of my most popular that I cook at home. Most of my friends make it all the time now, too. It's so delicious and healthy and packed with flavour. You will definitely want more, so I would recommend making double and packing leftovers for lunch the next day.

I like to serve this curry with brown basmati rice that's been rinsed and cooked with twice its volume of salted water. I frequently add a few cardamom pods, cloves and cinnamon bark to the rice to flavour it lightly. It complements the cloves in the sauce.

Prawn curry

Serves 2
1 tbsp cumin seeds
12 black peppercorns
4 cloves
2 tsp ground turmeric
1 onion, finely chopped
2.5cm fresh root ginger, finely chopped or grated
1 green chilli (more if you like it spicier)
1 tbsp light oil
2 garlic cloves, finely chopped
400g can chopped tomatoes
1 tsp caster sugar
400g can coconut milk
250g raw prawns, shelled and deveined
3 tbsp chopped coriander leaves
juice of ½ unwaxed lemon
sea salt
freshly ground black pepper

Fry the cumin for a minute in a dry frying pan and grind with the other whole spices in a mortar and pestle or spice grinder. Add the turmeric.

Fry the onion, ginger and chilli in the oil until the onion is soft and translucent. Tip in the garlic and fry for a couple of minutes. Add the spices and stir for a minute or so to temper them. Add the tomatoes and sugar and cook, stirring, for five minutes. Pour in the coconut milk, bring to a boil and cook for about 15 minutes, or until reduced by at least one-third. Add the prawns and cook until pink. It will only take a few minutes; take care not to overcook them.

Add the coriander and lemon juice to taste, to lift the flavour. Season and serve immediately.

I love calamari for supper. It's so quick, healthy and delicious. It is easy to source too, cheap and ethically sound as it's not over-fished in any way. I like to use smaller squid that are about six inches long and cut them into rings.

Calamari with tomato and green bean salad

Serves 2
3 tbsp extra virgin olive oil
1 tbsp balsamic vinegar
sea salt
freshly ground black pepper
100g cornmeal or polenta
2 squid, cleaned, cut into rings
200g green beans, topped and tailed
light oil, to deep-fry
250g cherry tomatoes, halved

Make the dressing by combining the olive oil and balsamic vinegar and stirring. Season to taste.

Place the cornmeal in a shallow bowl and season it. Toss the squid in the seasoned cornmeal and leave to the side.

Blanch the green beans in boiling water for three to four minutes until starting to soften but still firm. Run under cold water until cold, to stop the cooking.

Heat 5cm oil in a deep pan or a deep-fryer until it reaches 180°C on an oil thermometer, or a piece of bread froths the oil immediately when added. Fry the squid until starting to brown; no more than a couple of minutes. Drain on kitchen paper for a minute or so.

Toss the green beans gently with the tomatoes and the dressing. Serve the calamari on top and eat while warm.

Laksa is a fabulous soupy dish, fresh and lively, spiked with spices, aromatic with lemon grass, sour with tamarind and sweet and fruity with tomatoes. There are many types specific to parts of Malaysia and everyone has their own. This is one I came up with after much experimentation. I like to use salmon or prawns, although chicken would work too. It is difficult to get wild salmon these days, but farmed organic can work very well.

Salmon laksa

Serves 2
15g tamarind paste
100g rice vermicelli noodles
500ml light chicken or fish stock
50ml sesame oil
1 quantity Laksa Paste (see below)
250g ripe tomatoes, peeled and chopped
400g can coconut milk

250g salmon fillet, skinned,
   in 2.5cm chunks
1 red pepper, finely sliced
1 tbsp fish sauce
50g beansprouts
handful of mint leaves
4 spring onions, finely sliced
1 lime, quartered

A few hours before you eat, dissolve the tamarind in 200ml hot water, breaking it up with a fork. Cook the noodles according to the packet instructions, then arrest the cooking by running under cold water. Set aside. Strain the tamarind liquid into the stock after it has been soaked.

   Add the sesame oil to the laksa paste. Heat in a saucepan for a minute or so. Tip in the tomatoes and stir for five minutes until it forms a thick paste. Mix in the stock and coconut milk. Bring to a boil and simmer for five minutes. Add the salmon and red pepper and simmer for a few minutes, or until the fish is cooked. Season with the fish sauce. Divide the noodles and beansprouts between two large bowls and ladle in the soup. Top with mint and spring onions and serve with lime wedges.

LAKSA PASTE

1 tsp coriander seeds
1–2 red chillies, finely chopped
2.5cm chunk fresh root ginger,
   finely chopped
2 lemon grass stalks, trimmed, halved
   lengthways and finely chopped
3 garlic cloves, finely chopped
handful of coriander leaves

Toast the coriander seeds in a dry frying pan for a minute. Grind in a mortar and pestle or blender with the chillies, ginger, lemon grass, garlic and coriander to form a paste.

Growing up in Ireland, I thought that eating crabs was plain insane. Our elderly neighbour used to catch enormous ones in a bucket at a rocky beach near our house and boil them up for her Alsatian dog. I envy that dog now, but at the time I felt it was an act of cruelty. I was also terrified she would come near me with her bucket of living, sideways-walking friends. I was afraid of crabs, and really anything living in the sea. I remember standing on an isolated rock shrieking with horror as the crabs ascended. I thought that they would eat me. Of course they didn't, but I eat them now.

This is super-simple and a lovely expression of fresh crab. It benefits from the best ingredients, particularly the crab and the pasta. Bronze die pasta has a grainier surface – where the pasta has been extruded through a bronze die rather than the more common nylon – and so is better for clinging to sauces; it is also much more delicious.

Crab linguine with chilli, parsley and lemon

Serves 2
300g linguine
nice fruity extra virgin olive oil
1 red chilli, deseeded and finely chopped
150g white crab meat
finely grated zest and juice of ½ unwaxed lemon
handful of flat leaf parsley, chopped
sea salt
freshly ground black pepper

Cook your linguine according to the packet instructions so that it's just shy of al dente (it will cook a little more when you add it to the crab).

Heat about 2 tbsp of the oil, add the chilli and stir for about 30 seconds. Add the crab and stir until it's nice and hot.

Add the linguine to the crab and chilli and stir through, ensuring that the pasta is nicely coated; drizzle with some more oil if it's dry.

Add lemon juice to taste and some lemon zest with the parsley. Season to taste and serve immediately.

This recipe is a traditional Sardinian dish that is like the seaside on your plate. Fregola is a small, hand-shaped Sardinian pasta, which to me look like miniature bronzed pebbles on the beach. It is exceptional with vongole and fruity tomatoes and also very good with fresh cheeses. It's an obscure ingredient but a really good one so I wanted to include it in my book. It is increasingly available in good Italian delis and is easily sourced online, too. You can substitute with Israeli couscous if you can't get it, or another small pasta shape. Palourde clams are available in fishmongers and good supermarkets.

Fregola Sarda with vongole

Serves 2
600g palourde/carpetshell clams
sea salt
2 garlic cloves, finely chopped
300g baby plum tomatoes, quartered, or large tomatoes,
    peeled, deseeded and chopped
2 tbsp extra virgin olive oil
500ml light stock, such as chicken or vegetable
75g fregola Sarda
handful of flat leaf parsley, chopped
freshly ground black pepper

Cover the clams with some salted water for 10 minutes, then rinse. This will allow any sand in the shell to come out. Throw away any open clams that don't close when you tap them; these are dead, won't taste good and will probably make you ill.

    While the clams are soaking, sauté the garlic and tomatoes in the oil, in a big pan which has a lid, over a medium-low heat for five minutes.

    Add the stock and the fregola and cook until the fregola is almost done (this will depend on your fregola, but no more than five minutes).

    Clatter in the rinsed clams and cover the pan for two minutes. The clams will have popped open. Discard any that are still closed.

    Stir through the parsley. Season to taste and serve immediately.

This is a healthy dish that takes minutes and is full of flavour. Good food that tastes great doesn't have to be torture! I like to use trout as it has a very delicate flavour and is really good with both the avocado in the guacamole and the lime. Trout is very reasonably priced and available virtually everywhere so there is no excuse, really.

Trout with chunky guacamole

Serves 2
For the chunky guacamole
2 ripe avocados
juice of ½ lime
3 spring onions, finely chopped
1 green chilli, deseeded and finely chopped
1 garlic clove, finely chopped
75g baby plum or cherry tomatoes, quartered
handful of coriander leaves, chopped
sea salt
freshly ground black pepper

For the fish
1 tbsp light oil
500g trout fillets

Peel and roughly chop the avocados. Add the lime quickly, or the avocado will discolour, then the spring onions, chilli and garlic. Mash roughly. Stir in the tomato and coriander and season to taste.

Heat the oil over a medium heat in a frying pan and cook the trout fillets for two minutes on each side, or until done.

Eat immediately with the guacamole.

Gremolata is lively and spritely and often served with a rich beef or veal ragu to lift the meaty intensity (see page 140). It stands up really well on its own, too, as a marinade and is terrific with both pork and chicken. It is really simple and very cheap to make, simply lemon zest (from unwaxed lemons; you don't want wax melting on to your lovely chicken), chopped parsley and garlic.

This is a favourite speedy supper of mine, marinated and roasted until crisp. Spatchcocking flattens the chicken, making it much quicker to cook. Marinate the chicken for a couple of hours if you can, or put it in before you go to work and it will be full of flavour by the time you get home. Leftovers make great salad fodder for the next day.

Spatchcocking a chicken is very easy: just cut out the backbone with poultry shears or a sharp knife and flatten it down, pressing on the breast bone with your palm. You will need to loosen some of the joints to make it completely flat; just jiggle them about a bit! Easier still is to get your butcher to do it for you.

Gremolata spatchcocked chicken

Serves 2
1 small chicken, spatchcocked
handful of flat leaf parsley, chopped
4 garlic cloves, finely chopped
finely grated zest of 1 unwaxed lemon
2 tbsp extra virgin olive oil
sea salt

Weigh the chicken, so you can calculate its cooking time later.

Combine the parsley, garlic, lemon zest and olive oil and add a pinch of sea salt. Rub into the spatchcocked chicken, cover and leave to marinate in the fridge for two hours (or more) if you can. Don't worry too much if you can't marinate it for too long. It will still taste great.

Preheat the oven to 200°C/400°F/gas mark 6. Return the chicken to room temperature. Cook for 15 minutes per 450g plus 15 minutes more, turning halfway through and finishing breast side up so it gets nice and crispy. Rest for 10 minutes, then serve.

Right now, as I type and you read, there are people all over Lisbon eating rotisserie chickens saturated in piri piri and painting on more with big thick brushes dripping in the marinade. In Lisbon they cook the chickens in a rotisserie after a long rest in the marinade. I don't have a rotisserie at home – I expect you don't either – so I roast mine instead and it is a great dish and a perfect weekend lunch. It's also a brilliant speedy supper when you focus on the thighs and legs of the chicken, as I do here.

Cooking chicken in vinegar is common in many cultures. Chicken in red wine vinegar is served in Lyonnaise bouchons (and it's delicious!). Chicken en escabeche is the Spanish/Mexican equivalent. I love this Portuguese recipe as it is lively with spice.

Piri piri is a chilli, also called bird's eye chilli, and very fiery. If it's too hot for you, substitute fewer, milder chillies, it will still taste great. Make life easier by making the marinade the night before and marinating your chicken overnight. It will seep through the skin and permeate the flesh, giving great flavour throughout and keeping it really moist. Then all you've got to do is chuck it in the oven and let it roast. The juices that collect make a terrific sauce, be sure to spoon them over the chicken as you serve it.

Piri piri chicken

Serves 2
2 chicken thighs, skin on
2 chicken legs, skin on

For the marinade
120ml red wine vinegar
80ml extra virgin olive oil
6 bird's eye chillies, deseeded and chopped
3 garlic cloves, finely chopped
1 tbsp thyme leaves

The day before, prick the chicken skin several times with a fork. Mix the ingredients for the marinade and massage it in so the chicken gets to know it! Cover and refrigerate overnight, if possible, for the best flavour.

Supper time: preheat the oven to 180°C/350°F/gas mark 4. Roast the chicken pieces, skin side up, for 30 minutes and check on them. They will likely need 10 more minutes and will be done when the skin is browning and slightly crisp (the marinade will prevent it getting really crisp, but it is worth the sacrifice). Serve the chicken with the marinade and juices spooned over it.

Tip: this makes a really terrific Sunday roast too, with a whole chicken marinated and roasted.

A herby twist on chicken Milanese, this can be fried or roasted. Fried will give a better crumb and will be marginally fattier. Roasted is still good and should keep your conscience at bay. Sage and lemon are perfect partners. Ensure your sage is finely shredded as it is quite strong. I like to use Japanese panko, a great dry crumb that is now easily available. Any breadcrumbs will do though.

Breaded lemon and sage chicken

Serves 2
2 chicken breasts, skinless and boneless
50g plain flour
sea salt
freshly ground black pepper
1 egg, beaten
50g breadcrumbs, or panko crumbs
1 tbsp fresh sage leaves, finely shredded
finely grated zest of 1 unwaxed lemon
50ml olive oil (optional)

Flatten the chicken with a meat hammer, if you have one, or a rolling pin, until it's about half as thick as when you started (about 1cm).

Set out three shallow bowls. Pour the flour into the first and season it well. Put the egg in the second and, in the third, mix the breadcrumbs, sage and lemon zest.

Dip the chicken in the flour, shaking off the excess, then into the egg, letting the excess drip off, and finally coat thoroughly in breadcrumbs. Repeat for the second piece of chicken.

To fry, heat the olive oil, if using, until a piece of bread starts to fizz and crisp immediately, then fry the chicken for three minutes or so on each side until brown.

To roast, preheat the oven to 200°C/400°F/gas mark 6. Place the chicken on an oiled dish and roast for 15–20 minutes, or until cooked through. You can test by cutting through the thickest part of the chicken; it should no longer be pink.

These pies are super, full-flavoured and bursting to get out from under the pastry. I use cooking chorizo and chicken thighs, as they have the best flavour and stay moist. I make these in 12x8.5cm cast-iron dishes.

Chicken and chorizo pie

Serves 4
15g unsalted butter, plus more for the dishes
1 tbsp olive oil
500g chicken (preferably thigh meat), diced
200g cooking chorizo, sliced
2 fat garlic cloves, finely chopped
1 mild red chilli, deseeded and finely chopped
400g can tomatoes
2 tsp Spanish paprika
sea salt
freshly ground black pepper
handful of flat leaf parsley, chopped
250g ready-rolled all-butter puff pastry
1 egg, beaten

Preheat the oven to 180°C/350°F/gas mark 4. Heat the butter and oil in a large sauté pan or saucepan over a medium heat, and sauté the chicken until it starts to brown. Remove the chicken and sauté the chorizo for a few minutes until it starts to release oil, then add the garlic and chilli for a minute or so, stirring to ensure it doesn't burn.

Add the tomatoes and paprika, return the chicken and bring to a boil. Reduce the heat to a low simmer for 10 minutes. Season to taste. Remove from the heat and stir in the parsley.

Cut lids from the pastry to fit each pie dish, using a dish as a guide. Butter each pie dish and divide the pie filling between each. Add the pastry lids, brush with the egg and cook for 20 minutes or so, or until delightfully crisp and brown.

Duck breast is a completely different meat to duck leg. Duck leg is best cooked until falling off the bone and is rich and juicy with fat (see right), while duck breast is perfect and delicate when cooked only until still rosy and pink. It takes no time to cook and is delicious with fruit (plums or cherries), herbs and spices (five spice, star anise or chilli). This recipe calls for a marinade and, as with all marinades, the longer you marinate the more you will benefit. Aim for two hours if you can.

Soy and spice duck breast

Serves 2
75ml soy sauce
50ml rice wine
2 tbsp honey
2 star anise
1 red chilli, finely chopped
2 garlic cloves, finely chopped
2.5cm fresh root ginger, finely chopped
3 cloves
1 large cinnamon stick, broken in pieces
sea salt
freshly ground black pepper
2 duck breasts, rinsed and wiped dry

Mix all the ingredients except the duck breasts and season to taste. Bash them about a little with a rolling pin or pestle to get the flavours talking to each other. Slash the duck breast through the skin at 1cm intervals, but not through the fat. Pour some boiling water over the skin and pat dry. This will allow some of the fat to run off.

Cover the duck with the marinade in a compact dish or a freezer bag and rub it in with your fingers. Cover and marinate in the fridge for as long as possible, at least two hours if you can, or overnight.

Wipe the marinade from the duck breasts and fry in a dry frying pan on a low to medium heat, skin side down, for eight to 10 minutes, to render most of the fat and crisp the skin. No oil is necessary, there's lots of fat in the duck already.

When the skin is crisped slightly, turn over and increase the heat to medium. Cook for a further five minutes or so, until the breast meat is light pink but cooked. Let rest for a couple of minutes.

Serve sliced on top of stir-fried pak choi, or noodles fried with sesame oil, coriander and spring onion.

I love roast duck legs. Relatively cheap and quick to roast, they are a perfect quick meal. I like to spice these as I do the breast but the approach is a little simpler, using just chilli powder and Chinese five spice.

Roast the duck legs on top of the potatoes so the potatoes absorb all the gorgeous and delicious fat. If you are watching what you eat you may prefer to roast the duck separately, although you will miss a lot of the joy of the dish. This screams comfort and winter, but don't be afraid to spruce it up for summer with a nice salad.

Spiced roast duck legs with potatoes and pancetta

Serves 2
2 duck legs
¼ tsp chilli powder
½ tsp five spice
2 slices pancetta, diced
350g potatoes, diced
handful of flat leaf parsley leaves, chopped
pinch of sea salt

Preheat the oven to 220°C/425°F/gas mark 7. Prick the duck legs all over with a fork. Combine the chilli powder and five spice and rub into the duck legs. Leave to the side.

Fry the pancetta in its own fat for a couple of minutes over a medium heat, until starting to crisp. Toss with the potatoes and place in a small, high-sided roasting pan with the duck legs on top.

Roast for 10 minutes to crisp the skin, then reduce the oven temperature to 190°C/375°F/gas mark 5 and cook for 40 minutes, when the duck legs should be cooked through. You can check by seeing if the meat is pulling away from the bone.

Remove the duck legs from the roasting tray and add the parsley to the potatoes and pancetta. Season with salt to taste. Leave to rest for five minutes, then serve the duck legs on top of the potatoes.

Sadly I have never been to Beijing, but I have been to Chinatown and this is where I learned of *jiaozi* or Beijing dumplings. Easy to reproduce at home, they are the most perfect comfort food.

I highly recommend making the wrappers at home – if you have time – with dumpling flour from Asian shops, it makes a difference. However, for a quick week day meal, ready-made dumpling or wonton wrappers are fine.

Beijing dumplings with chilli and soy dipping sauce

Serves 4

For the filling
450g minced pork
3 spring onions, finely chopped
1 garlic clove, finely chopped
handful of Chinese chives
   (or normal chives), finely chopped
I tbsp rice wine vinegar
½ tsp sesame oil
sea salt
freshly ground white pepper

For the wrappers
EITHER
1 small pack gyoza or wonton wrappers
OR
250g dumpling flour, or 225g plain flour
   mixed with 25g cornflour or rice flour,
   plus more to dust
pinch of salt

For the dip
100ml soy sauce
1 tsp chilli oil or 1 red chilli, finely chopped

Mix all the ingredients for the filling, cover and leave in the fridge while you make the dumpling wrappers. This will allow the flavours to integrate.

For the wrappers, combine the flour or flours, salt and 75ml water and mix. Knead for 10 minutes until shiny and elastic, or chuck in your mixer and let it do the work for five minutes. You may want to add more water or flour; you want a mixture that is firm without being too wet. Cover in cling film or put in a plastic bag for 30 minutes in the fridge.

Pull off little balls, smaller than a 10p piece, and roll on a floured work surface until as thin as you can get without tearing, each about 7.5cm in diameter. Mix together the ingredients for the dipping sauce.

Brush the edges of the wrappers lightly with water (not too much or they'll get soggy). Place a teaspoon of filling in the centre, fold in a half moon shape and press or pleat closed, ensuring they are sealed.

Steam in a steamer or bamboo steaming basket for best results. Otherwise, add to boiling water for a few minutes; they will be cooked two minutes after they float to the top. Serve hot with the dipping sauce.

We need to see more pork burgers and I can never have enough chorizo in my life, so I came up with the recipe for these lively patties. They are perfect eaten in crispy pitta breads with a little salad or in a Middle Eastern khobez flatbread. Simple, quick, delicious, what more do you need in a quick dinner? Answers on a postcard please.

Pork and chorizo burgers

Makes 4
For the burgers
75g cooking chorizo
1 garlic clove, very finely chopped
handful of flat leaf parsley, chopped
400g minced pork
sea salt
freshly ground black pepper
1 tbsp light oil

To serve
small pitta breads (or a wrap, bun or similar)
mayonnaise (homemade is best, see page 75)
rocket leaves, or similar salad leaf
chopped tomatoes (I use juicy small tomatoes)

Peel the skin from the chorizo and chop as finely as you can. Add the garlic, parsley and chorizo to the pork and mix thoroughly. Season with salt and pepper. Cook a small amount in a frying pan and eat to check the seasoning; adjust if necessary. Shape the mixture into four patties.

If you have a griddle, heat it until it's extremely hot. Otherwise use a frying pan. There's lots of fat in the pork so you won't need much oil. Fry on one side for four to five minutes and turn. Reduce the heat slightly and allow the burger to cook through. It should take up to 10 minutes. Check by cutting into one: if it's pink, it's not ready.

Serve in toasted pitta breads (or your bread of choice), with some mayonnaise, rocket and tomatoes.

I love sumac, a gorgeous Middle Eastern spice made from ground berries. Sour in flavour, it is especially terrific with lamb. It wakes up these sleepy little meatballs, cosy in their cinnamon tomato sauce, while the cumin gives a robust background flavour. Sumac is relatively easy to source these days, but if you are struggling it is easily available online. For a super-speedy supper, serve the meatballs on toast.

Sumac lamb meatballs with cucumber and tomato couscous

Serves 2

For the meatballs
1 tbsp cumin seeds
300g minced lamb
1 tbsp sumac
sea salt
freshly ground black pepper
2 tbsp light oil
2 garlic cloves, finely chopped
400g can good chopped tomatoes
1 large or 2 small cinnamon sticks
handful of coriander leaves, chopped

For the couscous
150g couscous
100g cherry tomatoes, halved
½ cucumber, quartered lengthways
    and finely sliced
2 tbsp extra virgin olive oil
juice of ½ unwaxed lemon

Toast the cumin seeds in a dry pan over a high heat for a minute and grind with a mortar and pestle or spice grinder. Add to the lamb with the sumac and mix thoroughly with your hands. Shape into small meatballs about 2.5cm in diameter. Season lightly and taste by frying off a small ball and adjusting where necessary. Fry the meatballs on all sides until brown in half the oil, in two batches if necessary. Leave to the side.

Sauté the garlic for 30 seconds in the remaining oil. Add the tomatoes and cinnamon and stir through. Add the meatballs and cook for 10 minutes until cooked through.

Meanwhile, cover the couscous with boiling water in a bowl and seal with cling film. After 10 minutes, when the water should have been absorbed, run a fork through to fluff it up. Mix with the tomato and cucumber and dress with the olive oil and lemon. Season to taste.

Season the meatball sauce and add the coriander, stirring through. Serve hot on top of the couscous salad.

This is a rich, moreish dish. Completely delicious, you will find yourself scooping any remaining sauce with some bread from the pan. It's reasonably quick and all the better if you use home-cooked chickpeas (see page 160); it's worth the effort if you can. This has got me through many a grim winter's day.

Chorizo and chickpea stew

Serves 4
50g pancetta
200g cooking chorizo, in 1cm chunks
1 garlic clove, finely chopped
400g can tomatoes
300g cooked chickpeas (home-cooked are best, see page 160),
    or 400g can chickpeas, drained and rinsed
handful of flat leaf parsley, roughly chopped

Sauté the pancetta and chorizo in a dry sauté pan over a medium heat for two minutes, until starting to crisp. Add the garlic and fry for a further minute.

Tip in the tomatoes and chickpeas and cook for 20 minutes. Loosen with some water if it starts to get too thick.

Add the parsley, stir through and serve warm with some bread.

This recipe is deceptively simple and has superb flavour. Don't be put off by the anchovies, as they cook they melt and all that is left is a gorgeously intense, savoury flavour that works brilliantly with the herbs and garlic. As always, marinate the meat for as long as you can; you will reap the benefits.

Herbed lamb cutlets with anchovy

Serves 2
6 lamb cutlets
1 tbsp finely chopped mint leaves

For the marinade
3 tbsp finely chopped rosemary needles
3 tbsp finely chopped mint leaves
3 anchovies, finely chopped
3 garlic cloves, finely chopped
4 tbsp extra virgin olive oil

The day before, combine all the ingredients for the marinade and massage into the cutlets. Cover, refrigerate and leave to marinate for as long as you can and for at least four hours, or overnight is ideal.
    Supper time: bring the lamb to room temperature. Fire up a chargrill or frying pan when you are ready to eat. There will be no need to oil the pan as there is plenty of oil on the lamb already. Fry for three to four minutes on each side for medium-rare. For larger chops, fry for a bit longer. Check their progress by cutting into one of the cutlets and taking a peek. You can also judge by checking how firm they are. Rare will feel really soft and well done very firm. You want it in the middle.
    Rest for a few minutes and serve sprinkled with mint.

I have my friend Rachel to thank for the idea for this recipe. We competed in a barbecue championship and I had my usual array of spices and a very good roast chilli and spice-based marinade, if I do say so myself! Rachel brought the idea of marinating some rump steak in lemon, bay and garlic. It was utterly delicious, really subtle and aromatic. I had to include it here.

Rump is a very nice cut and is relatively reasonable, too. It deals well with marinades and is great for the barbecue, but lovely for a speedy supper at home indoors, too.

Lemon, bay and garlic steak

Serves 2
2 x 300g rump steaks

For the marinade
4 fresh bay leaves
finely grated zest and juice of 2 unwaxed lemons
4 garlic cloves, coarsely chopped
3 tbsp extra virgin olive oil

The day before, combine all the ingredients for the marinade and massage into the steaks. Leave to marinate for at least four hours or overnight.

Supper time: bring the steaks to room temperature. If you have a chargrill use that, otherwise heat a frying pan until very hot. There is no need to oil the pan as there is plenty of oil in the marinade. Cook the steak for three to four minutes on either side for medium-rare.

This recipe was born of a neighbourhood hedgerow forage resulting in a lot of blackberries. I knew immediately what I wanted to do with them, combined with some rich aged balsamic vinegar they would be perfect with some venison I had in the fridge. They were and it was super-quick, so it has become a favourite in autumn.

With regard to the recipe for the sauce, this – like anything you cook – requires you to taste it. The volumes of each ingredient depend on the sweetness of the blackberries, the richness of your stock and the wine you use. It's very flexible, so feel free to adjust to your preference. Use a good balsamic if you can, as the sauce will benefit from the richness. Serve with some honest-to-goodness mashed potatoes.

Venison with blackberry and balsamic sauce

Serves 2
2 x 250g wild venison steaks
sea salt
freshly ground black pepper
2 tbsp light oil, such as rapeseed or sunflower

For the sauce
glass of red wine (rioja or something similarly
    full-bodied works, whatever you have)
125g blackberries
1 tbsp balsamic vinegar
250ml meat stock (veal or light beef are best,
    but chicken works too)
1 tsp honey, or to taste

Pour the wine into a pan over a high heat and burn off the alcohol (you will smell it in the air) for a couple of minutes. Add the blackberries, vinegar and stock and cook over a low heat for about 10 minutes until the blackberries are cooked and mushy. Add honey to taste. Keep warm.

Ensure your venison is at room temperature. Season the steaks on each side and rub with a small bit of oil. Heat a griddle or similar until extremely hot. For a good five minutes if you can.

Fry the steaks for two to three minutes on either side for rare (which is how you should eat good wild venison), three to four for medium, five to six for well done (but please don't do that!). Rest for five minutes to allow the juices to settle, then serve on top of the warm sauce.

Bavette is widely known in France but a bit of a well-kept secret cut here. It is commonly known as skirt or flank steak and regarded as cheap and not all that interesting. However, with a little work and time the day before, it can be really tender. It is also one of the most flavourful cuts of beef. It's still relatively cheap too, which is a bonus. That is, until everyone realises how good it is! Bavette is best served medium-rare as it gets very tough when cooked well.

Ask your butcher to trim it for you, removing the membranes. Miso bavette is popping up more and more now and it's so good you can see why! It is like a tenor serenading you from your plate, absolutely irresistible.

Miso-marinated bavette

Serves 2
2 x 300g bavette steaks, trimmed

For the marinade
2 tbsp miso
2 tbsp mirin
1 tbsp soy sauce
1 red chilli, deseeded and finely chopped
1 garlic clove, finely chopped
2.5cm fresh root ginger, peeled and finely chopped

The night before, tenderise the bavette by hammering with a meat hammer, or bashing with a rolling pin, until half the original thickness.

Combine all the ingredients for the marinade and massage into the meat. Cover, refrigerate and marinate overnight if possible, or for at least four hours.

Supper time: bring the steaks to room temperature. Heat a chargrill or frying pan until very hot. Brush excess marinade from the bavette – particularly any solid bits – and fry for three minutes on each side until medium rare. Rest for three to four minutes and serve sliced.

Long Weekends

Gorgeous, simple dishes to share with friends

Weekends are a joy, for lazing, grazing and hovering in your kitchen. The perfect time to feed friends. I like to have plenty of time to socialise with them, so I aim for low and slow cooking for the big dishes. Long roasts are ready by the time friends arrive so I can enjoy the evening with them. And don't confuse slow cooking with difficult cooking; these recipes really couldn't be easier and the results are sensational. Your friends will be very impressed.

Platters of food for sharing in the garden, or even in your tiny London flat in my case, make a perfect summer's evening. Most of the work is done in advance. When cooking with friends you probably want to show off a little bit. Some of the grazing recipes here are great with drinks, such as the pulled beef nachos, others as a prelude to dinner, such as the squid, others still great for snacking on, such as the chicken wings.

✦ PASSION ✦

Fresh cheese

Homemade cheese is a joy and so very easy. Fresh cheeses generally don't melt, but are good for cooking. One of my favourites is Indian paneer. The first time I made it many years ago, I was surprised and delighted with the flavour and texture and haven't used shop-bought since. It feels rubbery and flavourless by comparison.

To make a fresh cheese, all you do is bring milk to a boil and curdle it with acid (lemon juice, white vinegar, yogurt or buttermilk). The milk separates into curds and whey very quickly. Pour it through a muslin-lined sieve, drain briefly, tie in a ball and hang it from your kitchen tap to drain. Paneer is an everyday and very quick cheese. Ricotta (see overleaf) requires a more gentle process and you have to be mindful of its temperature. I like to lux it up a bit by adding cream to make it rich and delicious.

Make as much as you can, you might as well! These recipes are for two, but double up for four and so on. Use full-fat milk, or you will get a small amount of insipid cheese that isn't worth the time and effort. As with all things food, the best ingredients deliver the best results, so use the best milk and cream that you can find.

Homemade paneer

2 litres full-fat milk
juice of 1 unwaxed lemon (plus more in case you need it)
25cm muslin square

Bring the milk to a boil in a saucepan. Just as the milk has come to a boil, add the lemon and stir for a minute or so as the curds and whey separate (the milk will get really clumpy). If they are not separating, add a little more lemon juice. Take from the heat – if you continue cooking the milk will get an unpleasant taste – and pour into a sieve lined with the muslin. Tie the muslin around the cheese with string, and hang the ball over a saucepan from your tap to allow it to drain for 30 minutes or so. I am happy to use as is, however, if you want it flat, place a lid on top of it – weighted down with a bag of sugar or similar – for a further 30 minutes. It's ready to use and really delicious. If you don't use it all, store it for a couple of days under water in the fridge.

Continued . . .

✦ PASSION ✦

Italian ricotta is very easy to make at home and is much better than most shop-bought versions (unless you are buying an artisanal version). Ricotta means twice cooked. This refers to the fact that it is a way of using up any outstanding milk solids that are lurking in whey leftover from making another cheese. Cheesemakers would cook these milk solids for a second time, adding extra milk if necessary. This home version isn't twice cooked, but observing a little sensitivity with regards to its temperature results in a very similar cheese and this is how most homestyle ricotta is made.

Homemade ricotta

2 litres full-fat milk
250ml double cream
pinch of sea salt
kitchen thermometer
juice of 1 unwaxed lemon (plus more in case you need it)
25cm muslin square

Heat the milk, cream and salt gently to 85°C and remove from the heat. Add the lemon juice and stir gently for a minute or so until the curds and whey separate. Strain in a muslin-lined colander until most of the liquid is out, then leave to sit for half an hour. If you want a drier cheese (for instance, if you want to use it for ricotta pancakes or for a cake), let it sit for at least an hour.

This is a lovely and really simple dip. Use it to dip crudités, or on little toasts with goat's cheese, rosemary and roasted tomatoes. Add a bowl of Chunky Guacamole (see page 47) for a feast of veggie dips.

Artichoke cream

Enough for 6 as part of a spread
250g jarred or tinned artichokes, drained
1 tsp thyme leaves
25g Parmesan cheese, finely grated
50ml extra virgin olive oil, plus more if needed
sea salt
freshly ground black pepper

Blitz all the ingredients except the seasoning with a hand blender or in a food processor until it has a creamy consistency. Add more olive oil if required. Season to taste with salt and pepper.

Aubergine burned over an open flame is one of life's unexpected pleasures. The skin is charred beyond redemption but, when peeled, reveals a yielding, squidgy and very smoky flesh. This dip is perfect served with toasted strips of pitta or flatbread as a snack before dinner, or simply for afternoon grazing.

Smoky moutabal

Enough for 6 as part of a spread
1 large aubergine
juice of ½ unwaxed lemon
35ml extra virgin olive oil, plus more to serve
2 tbsp tahini
sea salt
seeds of ½ pomegranate

Toast the aubergine over a gas flame, turning with tongs, until the flesh is soft and the skin is burned. Allow to cool, then peel off the skin under a cold tap.

Mash the flesh and add the lemon juice, oil and tahini. Season with salt. Serve with the pomegranate seeds and a drizzle of oil on top.

Chorizo, white beans and rosemary go so well together, I thought I would try an alternative way of using them and came up with this. It was an instant hit. This is a smooth and fragrant dip, an unusual twist on hummus that is a perfect partner for fried chorizo on cocktail sticks. It is infinitely better with home-cooked beans (see page 160), but good canned beans will do if you're in a rush, or need a fix.

Cannellini bean dip with chorizo on sticks

Enough for 6 as part of a spread
For the dip
2 garlic cloves, finely chopped
40ml extra virgin olive oil, plus more if needed
300g cooked cannellini beans (homemade are best, see page 160),
    or 400g can cannellini beans, drained and rinsed
needles from 2 sprigs of rosemary, finely chopped
juice of ½ unwaxed lemon
sea salt

For the chorizo
400g chorizo, cut into 1cm chunks

Sauté the garlic over a medium heat in 1 tbsp of the olive oil. Combine with all the other ingredients except the salt and blend.

Add more olive oil if needed; it will depend on the consistency of your beans. Season to taste with salt, remembering that the chorizo is salty.

Sauté the chorizo in a dry frying pan until brown and crisping on both sides. Put each piece on a cocktail stick (or use fondue forks, if you have them) and serve with the dip.

Potato croquettes are a fond childhood memory. When we were teenagers my sister started making them with fresh herbs and I never looked back. Potato mash with herbs, breadcrumbed and deep-fried, what's not to love?

For something a little different I use mashed celeriac and roll it into small ping pong-sized balls to make really good snack food for friends. Celeriac is a little soggier than potato, but it does mash very well. However, my favourite way of doing these (and the quickest) is to cut the celeriac into chips before breadcrumbing and deep-frying, as I do here. They make perfect grazing food: different, unexpected and delicious.

Celeriac croquettes

Enough for 6–8 as part of a spread
1kg celeriac
100g breadcrumbs
1 egg, beaten
100g plain flour
sea salt
freshly ground black pepper
300ml light oil (groundnut or sunflower), to deep-fry

Cut the celeriac into chips about 1cm wide and 3cm long.

Place the breadcrumbs in a shallow dish, the egg in another and the flour in a third. Season the flour well.

Coat the celeriac chips first in the flour, then the egg, then the breadcrumbs.

Heat the oil in a deep pan, or deep fat fryer, until a cube of bread fizzes and browns quickly when added.

Fry the celeriac until the breadcrumbs brown, drain on kitchen paper and serve with Tarragon Mayonnaise (see opposite).

✦ PASSION ✦

Homemade mayonnaise

Homemade mayonnaise is really luxurious and very cheap to make, it's just egg yolks, vinegar or lemon juice, mustard and oil. It requires some concentration as the egg yolks can only absorb a few drops of oil at a time or they will split. However, it comes together a lot more quickly than you would expect and is really worth the effort. It is much easier to make with a mixer but you can do it by hand quite easily, too. Just make sure you have a large balloon whisk to make the process much more efficient.

I like to make this mayonnaise with rapeseed oil, but sometimes make it with half sunflower and half extra virgin olive oil. Extra virgin olive oil is far too strong on its own and will dominate. Tarragon is a perfect herb for this mayonnaise but, if you can't find it, use whatever you can get. Basil and mint will make a lovely summer mayonnaise with a tomato salad; rosemary and garlic mayonnaise is delicious with lamb; horseradish mayonnaise with beef. And that's without even mentioning roast garlic mayonnaise or smoked paprika mayonnaise with chips … are you drooling yet?

Tarragon mayonnaise with crudités

Makes about 300ml
2 large egg yolks
1 tsp Dijon mustard
1 tsp lemon juice
300ml rapeseed oil, or 150ml sunflower oil
and 150ml extra virgin olive oil
sea salt
1 tbsp chopped tarragon

Combine the egg yolks with the mustard and lemon juice and whisk until thickened. Add the oil, a drop at a time. After half is added, you can begin to pour it in a trickle. Season with salt and stir in the tarragon.

Serve with sliced, very fresh raw vegetables, such as peppers, carrots and celery.

Crab is a glorious, light and fresh ingredient. Super-healthy and wonderful with spices, it's perfect in a world of recipes. I love to make bite-sized chilli crab cakes for snacking on with friends. They are really easy and very tasty; the perfect solution for an afternoon or evening's entertaining.

The easiest and quickest way is to buy ready-prepared crab meat from your fishmonger. Do feel free to tackle a crab yourself though, it's very satisfying, though it takes time, and it's cheaper.

Chilli crab cakes

Serves 4, or 6–8 as part of a spread
1 red chilli, deseeded and finely chopped
500ml light oil, to deep-fry, plus 1 tbsp
1 garlic clove, finely chopped
500g white crab meat
100g mashed potato (with no butter or milk added)
handful of mint leaves, finely chopped
handful of coriander leaves, finely chopped
3 spring onions, finely shredded
2 eggs, beaten
100g plain flour
sea salt
freshly ground black pepper
100g breadcrumbs

Sauté the chilli over a low heat in the 1 tbsp oil for three to four minutes until starting to soften. Add the garlic for a minute.

Combine with the crab, mashed potato, herbs, spring onions and one of the eggs. Shape into small balls about the size of a ping pong ball.

Place the flour in a shallow bowl and season it well. Place the second egg in another bowl and the breadcrumbs in a third. Dip each crab cake into the seasoned flour, then the egg, then the breadcrumbs.

Heat 5cm oil in a very large pan, or a deep fat fryer, until it reaches 180°C on an oil thermometer, or a piece of bread froths the oil when added. Fry the cakes in batches, drain on kitchen paper and serve warm.

Tip: these are lovely with lime mayonnaise. Follow the recipe for Lemon Mayonnaise (see page 106), substituting lime for the lemon.

I love gravlax, but I hate dill. Now there's a conundrum! So I looked at alternative ways of making it and especially for other greenery that would love salmon and go well in a gravlax. The Japanese love fish as much as the Scandinavians so I thought about doing a Japanese version and, after having a little play, hit on shiso and sake gravlax.

You may be asking what any of that is and, if you are, I apologise! I tend to get ahead of myself. Gravlax is salmon cured with equal amounts of sugar and salt, with alcohol and other stuff like beetroot (very common because it is delicious). The Scandinavians often sneak some dill in there, too. It's super-easy – it just takes time – and will impress. Serve it with some good bread and you and your guests will be very happy.

Choose the best and freshest salmon you can get. Wild is best when in season but can be hard to come by, so don't worry too much about that. Good farmed organic salmon will do very well. You'll need to start the recipe three days before you need it.

Japanese gravlax

Serves 8–10
50g caster sugar
50g sea salt
2 tbsp shredded shiso leaves
1kg salmon fillet, skin on
2 tbsp sake

Spread the sugar, salt and shiso on the salmon and gently rub it into both sides. Sprinkle the sake on top. Place in a lidded container and store in the fridge for three days.

Morning and evening, baste the gravlax with the juices that collect around it. It is ready on the third day.

Wipe the marinade from the fish, slice it thinly and serve with crackers or good bread.

I love crispy squid, especially this version. I like it a little intense so use fiery, numbing Sichuan pepper, but feel free to use just black pepper if you don't want the same effect.

Squid is cheap, sustainable and easy to source. It also cooks super-quickly. Have your fishmonger prepare it for you if you don't think you can face it.

Salt and pepper squid

Serves 4–6 as a starter, or 6–8 as part of a spread
75g plain flour
75g cornflour
1 tbsp Sichuan peppercorns, coarsely ground
1 tbsp black peppercorns, coarsely ground
1 tbsp sea salt
2 squid, cleaned, bodies cut into chunks, tentacles left whole
light oil, such as sunflower, to deep-fry

Combine all the ingredients except the squid and oil and mix thoroughly. Place in a shallow bowl and toss through the squid.

Heat 5cm oil in a very large pan, or a deep fat fryer, until it either reaches 180°C on an oil thermometer or a piece of bread froths the oil immediately when added. Fry the squid until starting to brown; no more than a couple of minutes.

Drain on kitchen paper and serve hot.

Chicken wings are delicious and, like a lot of delicious things, really cheap. They are perfectly moist as all the flesh is near the bone and, with so much lovely crispy skin covering it, what more do you need? I urge you to do yourself a favour and fry them. Not every day, just once in a while as a treat. They're good baked too and healthier, but fried is impossible to beat. As every high street in the UK will testify.

A note on breaking the wings. I prefer to do this as it makes them perfect finger food. Pop them with your hands by forcefully pulling at either end. Then sever the skin and flesh at the joint.

Crispy pomegranate molasses chicken wings

Serves 6–8 as a snack
For the marinade
150ml pomegranate molasses
1 tbsp cumin seeds, toasted and ground
1 tbsp coriander seeds, toasted and ground
1 tsp cayenne pepper
3 garlic cloves, finely chopped
75ml olive oil
½ tsp sea salt

For the chicken
1kg chicken wings, cut in half at the joint
2 whole eggs, or 3 egg whites, beaten

light oil, to deep-fry (groundnut
    or sunflower)

For the seasoned flour
300g plain flour
sea salt
freshly ground black pepper
1 tsp cumin seeds, toasted and ground
½ tsp chilli powder

Combine all the ingredients for the marinade and massage into the wings. Cover and leave in the fridge for at least two hours, preferably overnight. The next day, tip all the ingredients for the seasoned flour into a large polythene bag. Add the chicken, close the bag and toss.

Place the eggs or egg whites in a large shallow dish. Transfer the chicken to the egg, coat thoroughly, then repeat with the flour. Heat 5cm oil in a very large pan, or a deep fat fryer, until it reaches 180°C on an oil thermometer or a cube of bread froths the oil immediately. Fry the chicken in batches, ensuring the pan is not crowded. Drain on kitchen paper and serve warm.

Tip: to make a tahini dip to serve with the wings, roughly chop 3 garlic cloves and crush in a mortar and pestle with a pinch of sea salt and 1 tsp toasted cumin seeds. Add 175ml tahini paste, 50ml extra virgin olive oil and 75ml water. Add the juice of an unwaxed lemon until the taste and consistency suits you. Stir in chopped coriander leaves and serve.

This pulled beef is fantastic, robust, full-flavoured food for sharing, but you may choose to eat it on some polenta before it ever graces a plate of tortilla chips. Your choice.

It is a great recipe. Of course all of the recipes in this book are, but this has something really special, a rich, deep, lively flavour and great texture. The sauce is almost chocolatey rich, although don't let that put you off. It eats really well piled on top of polenta, but is great with the cheesy nachos, sour cream and tomatoes here, too.

A note on brisket, it's a terrific cut and very cheap. Why it isn't on every menu, I just don't know! When cooked slowly it pulls apart gently. You can't possibly overcook it, as long as you don't have it on a high heat.

Pulled beef nachos

Serves 8
For the beef
1.5kg brisket, ideally on the bone
   (1.3kg off the bone)
2 tbsp light oil
1 onion, finely chopped
3 garlic cloves, finely chopped
1 tbsp cumin seeds, toasted and ground
1 tsp coriander seeds, toasted and ground
1 tbsp chipotle chile flakes (or normal
   chilli flakes if you can't get them)
50ml cider vinegar
30g molasses, or 50g dark brown sugar

400g can tomatoes
2 bay leaves
500ml chicken or light beef stock

For the nachos
100g plain tortilla chips
150g good mild melting cheese such as
   light Cheddar, grated
150g good cherry tomatoes, quartered
1 tbsp extra virgin olive oil
150ml sour cream
handful of coriander leaves, chopped

Preheat your oven to 150°C/300°F/gas mark 2. Brown the brisket all over in 1 tbsp of oil over a medium heat, in an ovenproof casserole or frying pan that fits the brisket. Remove from the pan and leave to the side.

Saute the onion in the remaining oil over a medium heat for three or four minutes, stirring so it doesn't burn. Add the garlic for a minute.

Add the cumin, coriander and chipotle and cook for two minutes. Your kitchen should be smelling really good now! Pour in the vinegar, molasses, tomatoes, bay leaves and stock. Stir and cook for five minutes. Return the brisket. Cover loosely with foil: you want to protect the meat, but also to reduce the sauce. Place in the oven. After 1½ hours turn the brisket. Cook for a further 2–2½ hours until the brisket falls off the bone. Rest for 10 minutes, then shred the meat with two forks and mix with the sauce.

Spread the tortilla chips over a large plate and sprinkle with the cheese. Place under a hot grill to melt the cheese. Toss the tomatoes with the olive oil. Spoon tomatoes, sour cream and brisket over the tortilla chips and sprinkle with coriander leaves. Serve immediately.

A traditional Spanish tapa, this translates very easily to any domestic kitchen. It's a great one to knock up for unexpected guests, or for quick snacks. The cider reduces into a sticky sauce which is lovely with the bold chorizo. Cooking/fresh chorizo is best for this, but cured chorizo is fine too.

Chorizo in cider

Serves 4 as a starter with good toast, or 4–6 as part of a spread
500g chorizo, in 5mm slices
2 garlic cloves, finely chopped
200ml cider

Sauté the chorizo in its own oil over a medium heat until crispy on both sides. Add the garlic for a couple of minutes, then pour in the cider.

Reduce the cider by half and serve the chorizo on a plate with cocktail sticks and some good bread to mop up the juices.

These are perfect grazing food, served on bamboo skewers. Make them as big or as small as you like and serve in piles. The hot, charred, gently spiced koftes are lovely with the cooling tzatziki dip. This is a very quick dish too and you can make both koftes and tzatziki in advance and keep refrigerated until you need them. Best cooked on the barbecue, they will also cook well on the chargrill or under the grill. You will need eight bamboo skewers (or more if you are making smaller koftes).

Turkish lamb koftes with a quick tzatziki

Makes 8 large koftes
For the koftes
1 tbsp cumin seeds
1 tbsp coriander seeds
900g best minced lamb
1 red onion, finely chopped
3 garlic cloves, finely chopped
1 tsp chilli flakes (or more if you like things hot)
handful of flat leaf parsley, chopped

For the tzatziki
500g Greek yogurt
1 large cucumber, peeled, deseeded and grated
handful of fresh mint leaves, shredded

Soak the bamboo skewers in cold water for 30 minutes, to ensure they don't burn when you put them on the barbecue or under the grill.

Put the cumin and coriander seeds into a dry frying pan and place over a medium heat. Stir until they smell aromatic and have turned a shade darker. Tip into a mortar and grind to a powder with the pestle.

Combine all the ingredients for the koftes and mix well. Divide into eight portions and mould into sausages around the bamboo skewers.

Cover and refrigerate for an hour to firm up, or until you are ready to cook them.

Combine all the ingredients for the tzatziki and store covered in the fridge until ready to cook.

Cook the koftes over a barbecue, on a chargrill or under the grill, turning until browned on all sides. Serve with the tzatziki.

Lunch

Lunch may be light on preparation time and even portion size, but never in flavour. Ordinarily, lunches should be spritely. They should wake you up, not slow you down. They need to feed and fuel you to dinner, which is a far more serious and intense affair. These light, lively lunches form the first half of this chapter.

However there are exceptions here which are suitable for bitterly cold weather, especially after a brisk walk through the frost. These heartier lunches, complete with side dishes, make up the second half of this chapter. But even those recipes that are heavier on meat usually contain light and fruity elements, sharp vinegar or fiery spices.

Most recipes are quick, a few are a little more fiddly, but I promise they are all worth it.

Homemade bread

Homemade bread is worth making just for that fantastic aroma in your home. It really isn't difficult. The ingredients are simple: flour, water, salt and either yeast or a starter. All you do is introduce them to each other, encourage them to work together through kneading, let them bed in by allowing them to prove, then bake your lovely loaf.

Brown soda bread

Makes a 20cm round loaf
25g unsalted butter, diced
500g wholemeal flour, plus more to dust
100g oatmeal
1 tsp sea salt
1 tsp bicarbonate of soda
450ml buttermilk

Preheat the oven to 200°C/400°F/gas mark 6.

Add the butter to the dry ingredients and rub in with your fingers until the mixture resembles breadcrumbs. Add the buttermilk and mix.

Turn out on to a floured baking tray and create a round about 20cm in diameter. Cut a deep cross in the bread.

Bake for 30–35 minutes. The bread will be cooked when, if turned upside down and tapped, it sounds hollow.

Cool on a wire tray, covered with a clean, dry tea towel.

Sourdough bread

Sourdough bread is surrounded by myth but it's really very simple. It's a way of capturing and using the wild yeasts that grow on flour and exist in the air. It results in a rich flavour that develops slowly and is worth the time and effort. Everyone has their own approach and everyone knows best. Some use rhubarb in their starter; Julia Child used grapes. At home, I simply use flour allowed to ferment with water for a week or so.

It takes a little effort, as you have to feed the starter regularly with flour and water, but the rewards are rich. Artisan baker Tom Herbert gave me a tip recently for those days when you have lots of starter and no time to make bread. The answer is to make sourdough pancakes, using 250g starter, 75g sugar and an egg. They are the perfect combination of sweet and sour and I confess I make more of these than I do bread!

Basic sourdough starter

250g wholewheat flour

Mix the flour and 200ml hand-hot water thoroughly and knead for eight to 10 minutes. Place in a Kilner jar in a warm place and leave for three days.

Feed your starter daily by throwing away half, then thoroughly stirring through 150g wholewheat flour and 150ml water. When it starts bubbling it is alive (it's alive!) and is ready to use. Instead of throwing half away now, you can use it for bread or pancakes.

Basic sourdough bread

Sourdough is all about the starter, there is no need to complicate it further by using a tricky bread recipe. I prefer to keep it really simple. As you get to know your sourdough, tenderly and lovingly feeding it and watching the taste develop, you will most likely choose to expand on this recipe. It is a great starting point though and will provide you with a good, flavourful loaf. Sourdough keeps for up to a week so it will provide plentiful toast for breakfasts when it's no longer at its fresh best.

Makes 1 medium loaf
600g strong white flour
10g sea salt
150g alive sourdough starter

Put your flour and salt in a large bowl, create a well in the centre and slowly add 300ml water, mixing it in as you do. Then slowly add the sourdough starter. Mix with your hands, ensuring that it is well combined.

Knead thoroughly for 10–15 minutes (this depends on how much you put into it and how big you are!), until elastic and slightly shiny. Or mix in a food mixer with a dough hook to get the same result. It will take some time, but frees you up to do other things.

Put in a bowl and cover with a damp tea towel. Store in a warm dark area – an airing cupboard is ideal – until doubled in size. The time this takes depends on how active your starter is, but check it after an hour. Knock it back by punching the air out. Knead again for a few minutes. Shape into a large loaf, seam at the bottom (I make it quite round), and leave for a further hour. Preheat the oven to 180°C/350°F/gas mark 4.

Cut some slashes in the top of the loaf with a knife and bake for 35–40 minutes until a crust has formed and you get a hollow sound when you tap on the bottom.

Tip: for a good crust, spray some water into the oven after you add the bread. Also, bake on a pizza stone or tile to get a great, crispy bottom.

Blaas are a terrific bread roll from Waterford, where I am from. They are the only indigenous Irish yeast bread and are a source of county pride. We love them. A blaa is a fluffy white bread roll with a floury top, so expect to get a flour moustache as you eat them. This is my interpretation of blaas. For perfect blaas, such as those you would get in Waterford, make sure the rolls are baked very close together so when baked they join and you get soft sides when you pull them apart. I often make mine in a larger tray to get more crust, which doesn't look exactly like a blaa but still has the great flavour. Both ways work well. I sold very many of these when I had my stall at Covent Garden Real Food Market as it's the perfect vehicle for a roast meat roll and – dare I say it – a crisp sandwich. Especially with my beloved Irish cheese and onion Taytos.

Blaas

Makes 8
10g active dried yeast
10g caster sugar
500g extra strong white flour, plus more to dust
10g sea salt
10g unsalted butter

Dissolve the yeast and sugar in 275ml lukewarm water. Ensure that the water is warm, not cold or hot. Leave for 10 minutes. It should get nice and frothy, indicating that the yeast is alive and well.

Sift together the flour and salt, to introduce air. Rub in the butter. Add the wet to the dry ingredients and mix until combined. Knead for about 10 minutes, until the dough is smooth and elastic. It will go from rough to a little shiny.

Place in a bowl, cover with cling film, and leave in a warm place for 45 minutes. Remove from the bowl and knock back, pushing the air out the dough. Rest for 15 minutes, to give the gluten time to relax; this will make shaping easier.

Divide the dough into eight pieces. Roll each piece into a ball. Rest for five minutes more, covered.

Dust a baking dish with flour and place in the balls, side by side. Dredge with flour. Leave in a warm place for 50 minutes. Nearly there! Preheat the oven to 210°C/410°F/gas mark 6½. Dredge the blaas with flour for a final time and bake for 15–20 minutes.

Wild garlic and potato soup

Wild Garlic Pesto with Flowers (see below), glamorises a simple bowl of potato soup.

Serves 4
2 small onions, finely chopped
1 tbsp light oil
600ml good chicken or vegetable stock
2 fresh bay leaves
450g potatoes, diced
400ml full-fat milk
sea salt
freshly ground black pepper
2 tbsp Wild Garlic Pesto with Flowers (see below)
1 tbsp olive oil
a few wild garlic flowers

Sauté the onions in the light oil over a medium–low heat until starting to soften and become translucent. Add the stock, bay leaves and potatoes and bring to a boil. Reduce the heat to a simmer and cook until the potatoes soften (10–15 minutes). Add the milk and bring to a boil. Remove the bay leaves and blend. Season to taste.

Add half the pesto and stir through the soup. Mix the remaining pesto with the olive oil and swirl on top of each bowl, adding the deliciously oniony wild garlic flowers.

Wild garlic pesto with flowers

Makes about 600g
200g wild garlic leaves and flowers
75g Parmesan cheese, grated
75g walnuts
150ml extra virgin olive oil, plus more to store
juice of ½ unwaxed lemon
sea salt
freshly ground black pepper

Blitz all the ingredients in a blender. Season and store in the fridge under a film of oil.

So, you're wondering why there are so many potato soups … and why so much milk? My Irish background chooses these and they are so comforting. I love dishes that have a simple basis with something else to liven them up. Chive flowers grow in a big pompom ball, each one has many flowers. Pull them apart with your hands and you will be surprised at the delicate little flowers that form such a big ball of purple oniony intensity.

Potato soup with chive flowers

Serves 4
2 small onions, finely chopped
1 tbsp light oil
600ml good chicken or vegetable stock
2 sprigs of thyme
2 fresh bay leaves
450g potatoes, diced
400ml full-fat milk
sea salt
freshly ground black pepper
handful of chives
100ml extra virgin olive oil
handful of chive flowers taken from 2 big flower balls

Sauté the onions in the light oil over a medium-low heat for up to 10 minutes, until starting to soften and become translucent.

Add the stock, thyme, bay leaves and potatoes and bring to a boil. Reduce the heat to a simmer and cook for 10–15 minutes, until the potatoes are starting to soften. Add the milk and bring to a boil again. Remove the bay leaves and thyme sprigs and blend. Season to taste.

Meanwhile, blend the chives with the extra virgin olive oil to get a green oil. Serve the soup in bowls, sprinkled with chive flowers and a drizzle of the chive oil.

Salsify is a rough, pointy-looking vegetable that you'd be forgiven for walking past in the shop. However, underneath that murky rough exterior lies a creamy white, rich and delicious root vegetable. It takes a bit of work but is worth it. Called the oyster of the vegetable world (although it really isn't fishy!), it is a natural partner for cream and wonderful in a simple gratin. When I am not using it in this way, I like to partner it with mellow, nutty roast garlic in this lovely soup. Salsify is a bit fiddly, so save this for a special occasion or lovely dinner for two.

Salsify and roast garlic soup

Serves 2
700g salsify, unpeeled
squeeze of lemon juice
1 garlic bulb
extra virgin olive oil
2 large or 4 small shallots, finely chopped
1 tbsp olive oil
1 carrot, diced
1 potato, diced
2 litres light chicken stock
2 bay leaves
a few sprigs of thyme, plus more to serve
100g red lentils
sea salt
freshly ground black pepper

Scrub, scrub, scrub that salsify. Peel carefully, taking care not to strip too much of the flesh away. Chop into 2.5cm sections and drop into a bowl of water with a squeeze of lemon added, so it doesn't discolour.

To roast the garlic, preheat the oven to 180°C/350°F/gas mark 4. Slice the top from the garlic bulb, exposing the top of each clove and drizzle with extra virgin olive oil. Roast for 20 minutes and allow to cool, then squeeze each clove out of its papery jacket. I adore roast garlic. It should really have a chapter all of its own.

Sauté the shallots in the olive oil until translucent. Add the carrot and potato for a couple of minutes. Then add the stock, bay leaves, thyme, roast garlic, lentils and salsify.

Bring to a boil and simmer for 20 minutes or until the salsify is tender. Remove the thyme and bay, blitz in a blender and season to taste.

Serve sprinkled with thyme leaves and swirled with extra virgin olive oil. Cream would work really well, too, if you prefer.

✦ PASSION ✦

Cauliflower soup with spiced butter tortelloni

I owe the idea for this to one of my favourite London restaurants, Trinity. Spiced butter in a tortelloni melts when you boil it and, when you pierce it with your spoon, you are rewarded with a rush of gorgeous spicy butter. Homemade pasta is best and really not a trauma if you have a mixer. It is best rolled with a pasta machine as it is hard to get thin enough with a rolling pin … I have tried!

Serves 4

For the tortelloni
300g oo pasta flour
3 egg yolks
1 tbsp mustard seeds
1 tbsp cumin seeds
1 tsp coriander seeds
1 tsp chilli flakes
150g unsalted butter

For the soup
2 small onions, finely chopped
1 tbsp light oil
1 potato, diced
600ml good chicken or
    vegetable stock
400ml full-fat milk
400g cauliflower florets
2 fresh bay leaves

Put the flour in a bowl and create a well in the centre. Add the egg yolks and combine with a fork until a dough starts to form. Knead for 10 minutes until the dough becomes shiny and elastic. This is easier to do in a mixer with a dough hook. Wrap in cling film and rest in the fridge for at least 30 minutes. Dry-toast the spice seeds in a frying pan for a minute or so until they start to brown and pop. Grind in a mortar and pestle with the chilli and add to the butter. Combine well. Roll the pasta dough until very thin and cut into 10cm squares. Put a teaspoon of the butter in the centre and brush water around the edges. Press the edges until sealed then fold two of the corners together around your little finger and twist them to secure. Put in the fridge.

For the soup, sauté the onions in the oil over a medium-low heat for 10 minutes, until starting to soften and become translucent. Add the potato for a minute, then the stock, milk, cauliflower and bay leaves. Bring to a boil. Reduce the heat and simmer for 10 minutes until the potato and cauliflower are soft. Remove the bay and blend.

Boil some water and cook the tortelloni until a couple of minutes after they rise to the surface. Serve the soup in shallow bowls with three tortelloni per bowl of soup.

Pansies are delicious, pretty and not just whimsy. As well as brightening your dish they provide vitamins A and C. They are particularly good with melon, cucumber and lemon. I like to combine them here in a fresh and lively spring salad. This is great on its own but also good with a simple piece of white fish or chicken, or some feta to bulk it out.

Flower salad

Serves 4
12 pansies, different colours if possible
1 cucumber
½ honeydew melon
juice of ½ unwaxed lemon
3 tbsp extra virgin olive oil
150g cherry tomatoes, quartered
2 tbsp shredded mint leaves

Wash the pansies carefully, dry them gently and very well, then trim the stalks with a pair of scissors.

Slice the cucumber lengthways and remove the seeds by running a teaspoon down the centre. Cut each piece in half again, lengthways, then finely slice.

Peel and finely dice the melon.

In a small bowl, mix together the lemon juice and olive oil. Put the pansies, cucumber, melon and tomatoes in a salad bowl. Pour over the dressing and toss the salad just before serving, sprinkled with the mint.

Spelt is a grain that is very easy to digest, highly nutritious and lovely and nutty. It is used a lot in Italian cooking and increasingly so here. It is perfect for coeliacs – should you have one visiting or resident – and regardless makes a gorgeous summer salad bright with tomatoes, herbs and buffalo mozzarella. It's a great dish served on a big platter for sharing, with pitta bread on the side.

Spelt salad

Serves 2
200g pearled spelt
200g courgettes, quartered lengthways and finely chopped
1 tbsp light oil
2 garlic cloves, finely chopped
200g cherry tomatoes, quartered
250g ball buffalo mozzarella, torn into small chunks
2 tbsp shredded basil leaves
1 tbsp shredded mint leaves
1 tbsp good balsamic vinegar
3 tbsp fruity extra virgin olive oil
sea salt
freshly ground black pepper

Cook the spelt in boiling water for 15–20 minutes, until tender.

Meanwhile, sauté the courgettes in the light oil for four to five minutes over a medium heat until tender, then add the garlic and cook for a further two minutes. Allow both courgettes and spelt to cool.

Gently combine all the ingredients except the balsamic vinegar, olive oil and seasoning. Make the dressing by mixing the vinegar and oil. Dress the salad and season to taste. Serve immediately, as the dressing will make the salad soggy if left too long.

✦ PASSION ✦

———

Homemade wine vinegar

What to do with the ends of bottles of wine? If you ever have any, that is! Homemade wine vinegar is a bit of a revelation. We've all heard people moan that the wine in X restaurant was open too long and turned to vinegar. And they were right. Making your own vinegar can be complicated, there is bacteria you can buy and mother starters. As with most things though, there is an easier route that just takes a little more time.

Like most things that develop over time, such as sourdough bread and yogurt, a starter is required (called a 'mother' for vinegar). You can develop your own starter by leaving your wine in a warm place and just letting it happen. Air is required for wine to become vinegar, so don't store it in an airtight container but cover with a cork that is slightly ajar. Add more wine (making sure it is all either white or red, not both) as you have leftover bottles. After some time, it will become vinegar. This could take anything from a few weeks to a couple of months, but once you have developed your 'mother', making vinegar with it will take about a week.

To make a quick mother, you can combine your leftover wine with some cider vinegar to get it started. The flavour is better the long way though!

To make vinegar with your mother, you simply add leftover wine as you have it and it very quickly becomes an interesting new vinegar. As long as the wine was reasonably decent in the first place! Don't worry about proportions or amounts.

Homemade pizza

Homemade pizzas are a joy and so very easy. Even with the most expensive toppings they make a relatively cheap lunch. It's worth investing in a pizza stone, which should cost no more than £15. Pizzas need to be cooked at very hot temperatures and these little stone slabs, preheated in the oven before cooking, will ensure you have a perfectly crispy crust; the closest you will get to the results of a wood-fired or commercial oven.

Use fresh yeast, it gives a better flavour and texture and works more quickly. Some disagree and say you get the same results with dried yeast. It's not bad, it's true, so again don't worry too much if this is all you can get.

I consider myself to be a little bit of a pizza expert. I spent some time in Italy when younger and tried and learned lots, then came back and made many in a restaurant kitchen while at University. I used to curse making that daily enormous batch of dough, but now I look back fondly. Especially when I remember the boss going on holiday and telling the manager, 'Whatever you do, don't let her make that potato pizza she's always talking about'. You know what, I did. And it was really good.

For toppings, I have four favourites here (see opposite). Enjoy.

Pizza dough

Makes 8 25cm diameter bases
10g fresh yeast, or 5g dried yeast
25ml extra virgin olive oil, plus more to oil
10g salt (it's best to measure here, as an unseasoned dough is an unhappy one)
550g strong white flour, plus more to dust

It is easiest to use a mixer but I have made this by hand many times so don't worry too much if you don't have one. Measure 300ml warm water. You should be able to keep your hand in it with no problems – this is important – any hotter and you will kill the yeast; you only want to wake it up. Add the water to the fresh yeast and stir thoroughly. If using dried yeast, leave it for 10–15 minutes until it froths before proceeding. If using fresh yeast, add the oil and salt straight away then add to the flour, mixing as you do.

If using a mixer, knead on medium-high speed for 10 minutes until the dough has become elastic. You will notice it is stretchier and has taken on a sheen. You should be able to tease a ball of it with your fingers and look through it, without ripping it. By hand it's a more arduous task but very satisfying. It's the best thing to do after a rubbish day, I promise you! Knead vigorously on a floured surface for 10–15 minutes until you get to the same stage.

Place it in a high-sided bowl and cover with a clean tea towel or cling film. Leave in a warm place until doubled in size; it usually takes an hour or so. Knock back with your fists to knock the air out and leave to rise for about 10 minutes. It is now ready to use.

To shape, roll the dough into a long sausage, then divide into eight equal pieces. Cover with a tea towel or some lightly oiled cling film as you work with each piece.

You can roll these with a rolling pin but I prefer to mould them by hand as the rougher, more uneven results and lumps and bumps give a better texture. Just get your knuckles in and make a flat circle out of the dough about 5mm thick.

Spread over a couple of tablespoons of sauce, then lightly top the pizzas. Don't put on too much topping or they will be soggy and dense and go easy on the cheese. Use any cheese you like ... but please, no rubbery, cheap mozzarella.

Pizza sauce

I do pizza sauce one of two ways.

In the summer, when tomatoes are in season, I roast some tomatoes gently at 150°C/300°F/gas mark 2 for an hour or so, with some thyme, fresh chilli and garlic. When they are cool, remove the skins from large tomatoes and blitz in a blender.

In the winter, I use good canned tomatoes. First sauté a couple of finely chopped garlic cloves in olive oil for 30 seconds or so, then add one can of good tomatoes and 1 tbsp brown sugar. Good tomatoes? Yes. Better flavour, better everything, they are worth paying extra for. A pinch of dried chilli, or a small mild fresh chilli, is good here too. Let the sauce cool and add a handful of chopped basil leaves.

My four favourite toppings

Bufalina. Delicious in its simplicity, just sliced buffalo mozzarella on tomato sauce, with fresh tomato slices and torn basil leaves added after it is cooked.

Artichoke cream and goat's cheese. Add a few teaspoons of Artichoke Cream (see page 71) in dots around the pizza, with some goat's cheese of your choice in between. Finish with some grated cheese; I like pecorino or manchego here.

Parma ham. The quality of the ham speaks for the pizza, so use the best you can get and, if you can get it freshly sliced, it's usually cheaper and better. This pizza has tomato sauce, a little mozzarella cheese and then a few scattered slices of ham. Finish with rocket leaves when it's cooked.

That potato pizza. I know, potato pizza, eh? But it is traditional! I first saw it in a Roman pizzeria when I was but a young 19 and determinedly recreated it myself. Slice the potatoes very thinly (preferably using a mandolin) and top the pizza with the potatoes, fontina cheese and a little thyme or marjoram. Drizzle with extra virgin olive oil before baking so it doesn't get too dry. I love it!

I adore latkes, that delicious Jewish staple of shredded fried potato, like a mini rosti. Traditionally served with sour cream and apple sauce they are hard to beat, but I love this earthy beetroot interpretation. As with potato latkes, you need to squeeze the grated beetroot of all of its juices before adding the egg and shaping it into cakes. Horseradish is perfect with beetroot, you can add it to the latke as I do here, or to the sour cream if you prefer.

Beetroot latkes

Serves 2
5 raw beetroots, peeled and grated
5cm fresh horseradish root, peeled and finely grated,
    or 2 tbsp jarred grated horseradish
1 egg, beaten
sea salt
freshly ground black pepper
2 tbsp light oil
200ml sour cream

Squeeze all excess moisture out of the beetroot. It's easiest to do this with a clean tea towel, one whose colour you don't care for. Place the grated beetroot inside, roll and twist it until the towel is bright pink and the beetroot is as dry as you can get it.

Combine the dried beetroot with the horseradish, then the egg. Season, then shape into patties and shallow fry over a medium heat for a couple of minutes on each side in the light oil.

Serve with the sour cream.

✦ PASSION ✦

―――❖❖❖❖❖――――

Courgette flowers, giant couscous

When in season, it's reasonably easy to get your hands on courgette flowers. Ideally buy small courgettes with the female flower attached (the courgette is actually the fruit of the female flower). Male flowers are fine too, though in this case I would suggest battering only the flower and chargrilling the courgettes separately.

Serves 4
For the courgette flowers
12 small courgettes with flowers attached
(or 12 male flowers and 12 small courgettes)
150g ricotta (homemade is best, see page 70)
25g Parmesan cheese, finely grated
12 mint leaves, finely shredded
125g plain flour
2 tbsp cornflour
light oil, for deep-frying

For the salad
150g Israeli couscous (or normal couscous)
200g baby plum or cherry tomatoes, halved
1 red onion, halved, sliced into fine rings
handful of basil leaves, torn
leaves from 2 sprigs of mint, finely shredded
2 tbsp olive oil
juice of ½ unwaxed lemon
sea salt
freshly ground black pepper

Remove the bitter stamens from the flowers. Combine the ricotta, Parmesan and mint and put 1 tsp into each flower, folding the petals around. Cook the couscous according to the packet instructions. Toss with all the other salad ingredients.

Sift the flour and cornflour and stir in 200ml iced (preferably sparking) water with chopsticks or a knife, until it has the consistency of single cream. Don't worry about lumps, it's almost better to have them. Heat the oil in a pan until a piece of bread fizzes immediately. Fry the flowers and courgettes in batches; don't crowd the pan. Drain on kitchen paper and serve with the salad.

Aubergine is the meat of the vegetable world. It gets a bad rep as it can soak up lots of oil and is often ridiculously greasy. Cooked correctly this isn't a problem. Years ago, it was important to salt them to get rid of bitterness, but this is no longer necessary as they have been bred to exclude it. The myth still persists as an old wives' tale though.

I like to make little fritters, as squishy aubergine is perfect with a crisp crumb exterior. A nutty, sharp dressing is lovely with these. Scattered with jewel-like pomegranate seeds, it is a very pretty and delicious dish.

Crumbed aubergine fritters with pomegranate and tahini

Serves 2

For the tahini dressing
3 garlic cloves
1 tsp sea salt
50ml tahini
juice of ½ unwaxed lemon
freshly ground black pepper
1 tbsp finely chopped flat leaf parsley

For the aubergines
100g breadcrumbs
1 egg, beaten
100g plain flour
2 aubergines, in 5mm slices
300ml light oil, such as
    groundnut, to deep-fry
2 tbsp pomegranate molasses,
    plus more to serve
seeds from 1 small pomegranate

Make the dressing. Grind the garlic cloves and salt in a mortar and pestle until it becomes a paste. Beat the tahini, garlic and lemon, gradually adding water until you get a consistency that is like pouring cream. Season to taste and stir in the parsley. Set aside.

Place the breadcrumbs in a shallow dish, the egg in another and the flour in a third. Season the flour well. Dip the aubergine slices in the flour, then the egg and finally the breadcrumbs.

Heat the oil in a deep-sided frying pan, a wok or deep fat fryer, until a cube of bread starts to brown immediately (or a cube of aubergine!). Add a layer of your aubergine slices and fry for two to three minutes on each side, turning halfway through.

Drain on kitchen paper (the aubergine will have absorbed quite a bit of oil) and serve hot with a drizzle of the dressing, another of pomegranate molasses (just a little of this) and the pomegranate seeds.

Tip: this is delicious in pitta bread as a great alternative to a kebab for veggies, with some salad.

Labneh is the most simple fresh cheese. In fact it isn't a cheese at all, it is a simple strained yogurt. You need to use a thick Mediterranean-style yogurt – such as Greek yogurt – and all you do is strain it for several hours, overnight is best. You are left with a thick mass of yogurt that you can shape into little balls and marinade in flavoured oils, store in jars, or use in a spritely summer dish as I do here. This is a little sweet but is still a good lunch and epecially nice spread on some toast with a green salad.

Labneh with pistachio and rose

Serves 2
500g Greek yogurt
2 tsp rose water
75g shelled unsalted pistachio nuts, crushed

Make your labneh by lining a sieve with muslin and suspending it over a small saucepan. Add your yogurt and allow it to drain overnight in the fridge for up to 24 hours, the longer the better.

Shape the strained yogurt into little balls and arrange in two bowls.

Add 1 tsp of rose water to each and sprinkle with the crushed pistachio nuts.

Celeriac rémoulade is not very far removed from a coleslaw, but is somehow more elegant and delicate. Celeriac is a favourite vegetable of mine and it's very soothing to eat. Yes, it does look a bit crazy and aggressive but don't let the knobbly root turn you off, it's delicious!

Make it ahead to allow the celeriac to soften in the dressing. Homemade mayonnaise is best, but if you are stuck for time or can't be bothered, shop-bought is OK, too. This makes a great lunch with good ham, pickles and bread.

Celeriac rémoulade

Serves 4–6 as part of a spread
For the mayonnaise
2 large egg yolks
1 tsp white wine vinegar or cider vinegar
½ tsp sea salt
1 tsp Dijon mustard
300ml rapeseed oil, or other light oil

For the celeriac
1 celeriac
juice of ½ unwaxed lemon
1 tbsp Dijon mustard
handful of flat leaf parsley, chopped

Firstly, make your mayonnaise by combining the egg yolks with the vinegar, salt and mustard and whisking until creamy, then very slowly adding the oil as you whisk. Add the oil drop by drop initially so as not to split the egg yolks. This is easiest in a mixer, if possible.

Peel and chop the celeriac into matchstick-sized strips. Keep them covered with water to which the lemon juice has been added, so they don't discolour. Drain the celeriac very well after it has all been chopped and add the mayonnaise, mustard and parsley.

Stir and leave in the fridge for at least half an hour until the celeriac has softened a little.

Tip: this is also terrific in a sandwich with leftover roast pork.

Hot-smoked salmon is easy and very satisfying to make at home. Completely different to cold-smoked fish, it is cooked through but has a gorgeous smoky flavour. If you don't like the texture of cold smoked salmon, try this. I am sure you will love it. It's also a genius use for those leftover Christmas biscuit tins. You can of course buy hot-smoked salmon, but it is a lot of fun to make your own and the results are superior. I've also hot-smoked good double cream and made smoked butter, but that's another story …

All you have to do is drill some holes in the lid of a biscuit tin, then put untreated sawdust (try your local pet shop!) or some woodchips for smokers in the bottom, a wire rack on top of that (chicken wire will suffice if you don't have one that fits) and there you have it, a little hot smoker. Be warned, it does emit a lot of smoke, so use it outside if you can on a barbecue, or under a powerful extractor fan, or by an open window at least!

Hot-smoked salmon with lemon mayonnaise

Serves 2

For the lemon mayonnaise
2 large egg yolks
1 tsp Dijon mustard
½ tsp sea salt
finely grated zest and juice of 1 unwaxed lemon
250ml light oil, such as rapeseed, groundnut or sunflower

For the salmon
1 tbsp light olive oil
2 x 150g fillets wild or organic salmon, skin on

Make your mayonnaise first. Whisk the egg yolks with the mustard, salt and half the lemon juice until it becomes creamy. Slowly add the oil, initially a drop at a time then, after half has been added, in a dribble. This is to ensure that the egg yolks don't split. Add the remaining lemon juice and zest slowly at the end.

Set up your biscuit tin (see recipe introduction). Place the woodchips or sawdust in the bottom with the wire rack on top. Rub the oil on the salmon and place it on the rack, skin side down. Put the lid on and place the tin over a medium heat on your hob, or barbecue. Once you see smoke coming from the tin, it should take five to eight minutes to cook.

Remove from the tin and serve with the lemon mayonnaise and Brown Soda Bread (see page 86).

Diver-caught scallops are best for this, so ask your fishmonger for them. Dredged scallops destroy the sea bed, are full of sand and never taste as good. If possible get them in their shell with the roe attached and have your fishmonger remove them before you take both home. Samphire is a gorgeous, tender sea vegetable and is petite, salty and sweet. It reminds me a little of asparagus, in fact it is called sea asparagus in some parts of America. It's perfect with seafood.

Scallops with samphire and pancetta

Serves 4
4 thick slices of pancetta, cut into lardons
4 handfuls of samphire, soaked in water for 30 minutes, then drained
12 scallops

Sauté the pancetta until starting to crisp and add the samphire. Stir to ensure that it is coated in the pancetta fat, then add the scallops and cook for a couple of minutes on each side. You want them to be almost sashimi raw in the centre, that's when they taste best.

Eat immediately, preferably served in the scallop shells.

There are many ways to cook baby back ribs, those delicious racks of pork ribs, often very cheap and always under used (in the UK and Ireland at least, they are a big deal in the US). You can use a dry rub or a wet marinade, both allowed to mingle with the meat at least overnight; 24 hours is best. I like to use a wet marinade for this lunch recipe, a fruity, light tomato one. Most US recipes use catsup (it took me a little while to figure out that was ketchup!) but I use canned tomatoes instead, in the interests of keeping it light and fruity. Make as many as you can. This recipe serves four, but everyone wants more …

Baby back ribs

Serves 4
2 tbsp cumin seeds
1 cinnamon stick, broken
400g can good chopped tomatoes
50ml honey
50ml red wine vinegar
3 tbsp Worcestershire sauce
6 fresh bay leaves
2 chillies, finely chopped
2 racks baby back ribs (there is no point
    in making just one, you will regret it!)

The day before, tip the cumin seeds into a dry frying pan and place over a moderate heat, stirring, until aromatic and slightly darker. Pour into a mortar and grind to a powder with the pestle (or grind in a spice or coffee grinder).

Put the cumin into a pan with all the other ingredients except the pork ribs, and heat gently until well combined. Leave to cool. Pour into a large polythene food bag and add the ribs.

Seal the bag and massage the marinade well into the pork. Place in a large, shallow dish and refrigerate overnight, or for 24 hours if possible.

When ready to cook, bring the pork ribs to room temperature. Preheat the oven to 150°C/300°F/gas mark 2. Wrap the ribs in tin foil and roast gently for 2¼ hours.

Check that the ribs are pulling away from the bone; roast for a further 15 minutes if needed. Slice between the ribs with a sharp, heavy knife and serve hot.

I first had a salad like this on holiday in Granada and had to recreate it when I came home. It is so simple and makes the best of broad beans when in season. It is a little bit of a chore – OK a lot of a chore – but they are best double-podded, first removing the green pod and then the individual jackets. The sweet, gentle bean underneath is a gorgeous revelation. I like to use a Spanish jamón such as Serrano ham, but prosciutto will do too. As this recipe is Spanish I use a sherry vinegar in the dressing, which works best. Ham loves mustard, so I include some in the dressing with garlic to give it a punch.

Broad bean and ham salad

Serves 2
For the broad beans and ham
300g broad beans (double-podded weight)
125g jamón serrano or prosciutto, torn into pieces
handful of flat leaf parsley, chopped
freshly ground black pepper

For the dressing
1 tbsp sherry vinegar
3 tbsp extra virgin olive oil
1 garlic clove, finely chopped
1 tsp Dijon mustard
pinch of sea salt

Boil the broad beans for two to three minutes, then cool in iced water or under a cold running tap to stop them cooking further and to preserve the gorgeous bright green colour.

Whisk all the dressing ingredients together.

Combine the broad beans, ham and parsley and toss with the dressing. Season to taste and serve.

I love quail for many reasons, one of the main being that the ratio of skin to flesh is very high, so you get a lot of fabulous crispy skin. The slightly gamey flesh takes well to marinades and cooks super quickly. Try to find quail from a source you trust and avoid intensively farmed birds. Spatchcocked quail is quick to cook and easy to eat. The job is a little fiddly but quick: cut out the backbone, remove the attached bones and flatten the bird with the palm of your hand, pressing on its breastbone. It's easier to get your butcher to do it for you, but don't stress about doing it at home. I marinate it in many ways but this is one of my favourites. As always, I recommend you use fresh whole spices as you will see an enormous difference in flavour. I like to eat this with a bountiful leafy salad with a simple lemon dressing. This recipe is easy to scale up for friends.

Spiced quails with salad

Serves 2
For the quail
1 tbsp cumin seeds
1 tbsp sumac
1 tbsp thyme leaves
1 garlic clove, finely chopped
4 tbsp extra virgin olive oil
2 spatchcocked quails
sea salt

For the salad
1 round lettuce
handful of tomatoes, quartered
juice of ½ unwaxed lemon
3 tbsp extra virgin olive oil
freshly ground black pepper

Place the cumin seeds in a small dry frying pan over a high heat and stir until they smell fragrant and turn a shade darker. Tip into a mortar and pestle and grind to a powder. Combine with the sumac and thyme. Add the garlic and oil and rub all over the quails. Cover and chill for at least two hours, preferably four, or even overnight.

When ready to cook, bring the quails to room temperature, season with salt and preheat the oven to 200°C/400°F/gas mark 6. Roast the quails for 20 minutes; they should be cooked but moist and tender.

Wash and roughly tear the lettuce and toss with the tomatoes. Dress with the lemon and olive oil and season. Serve with the quails.

I love these delicate, glorious rolls, so light and fresh with their lively herbaceous filling. If you aren't familiar with them they look like delicious little pillows of flavour … and they are! These are also perfect for coeliac friends, as they are made from rice flour.

Rice paper wrappers are easier to come by now, large supermarkets and Asian food shops will stock them. They are a little fiddly, but with some practice come together in no time. You can always have your guests make their own for an interactive fun lunch.

If it's your first time making them, have some extra wrappers on hand as you may need to try a few before being happy with them. Larger wrappers are easier, too.

Vietnamese summer rolls

Serves 4
For the rolls
50g rice vermicelli noodles
300g pack Vietnamese rice paper wrappers
200g cooked prawns, shelled and deveined
1 red pepper, deseeded and finely sliced
½ cucumber, halved, deseeded and finely sliced
3 spring onions, shredded
50g beansprouts
handful of mint leaves, chopped
handful of coriander leaves, chopped
handful of Thai basil leaves, or normal basil leaves, chopped

For the dipping sauce
juice of 1 lime
4 tbsp fish sauce
2 tbsp rice vinegar
2 garlic cloves, finely chopped
1 red chilli, deseeded and finely chopped

Cook the vermicelli according to packet instructions and run under a cold tap to stop the cooking. Clear an area for making the rolls, you will need some elbow room! Fill a wide pan with water and soak each wrapper individually until soft, it won't take more than a minute.

In the centre third place three prawns and a little of each of the other ingredients. Not too much or it will be very difficult to roll. Fold the end facing you over the filling, then fold over the sides. Roll to the end and there you have it, a Vietnamese summer roll! Store the rolls under cling film in the fridge so that they don't dry out.

Mix the ingredients for the dipping sauce and serve it with the rolls.

These may be fried but they are really light and zesty with a bit of a kick. A gentler take on a spring roll (although they work really well with spring roll wrappers too), these summer rolls can be eaten fresh, but I can't resist frying them. Minced pork shoulder is best for this, it has the appropriate level of fat content and also has great flavour.

Lemon grass is great with pork and makes me think of sunshine and holidays. The stalks may look confusing; what to do with that? But when you remove the outer layers and finely chop the stems you have a fantastic, full-flavoured and aromatic ingredient. As such it is important not to use too much.

When you fry the rolls the meat crumbles, so when you bite in you find little pork crumbles fugitive among the noodles. I think I might have to run off and make some more now.

Fried aromatic pork summer rolls

Makes about 20 rolls
2 lemon grass stalks, trimmed
    and finely chopped
2 garlic cloves, finely chopped
1 red chilli, deseeded and finely chopped
2.5cm fresh root ginger, finely chopped
light oil, for deep-frying
400g minced pork shoulder,
    or best minced pork

50g rice vermicelli noodles
handful of mint leaves, chopped
handful of coriander leaves, chopped
3 spring onions, shredded
50g beansprouts
1 carrot, grated
300g pack Vietnamese rice paper
    wrappers (or spring roll wrappers)

Fry the lemon grass, garlic, chilli and ginger in 1 tsp of the oil for a couple of minutes. Add the pork and stir for about five minutes, until brown and cooked through. Meanwhile, cook the noodles according to the packet instructions, drain, then cool under a tap.

Arrange the ingredients in bowls or on a plate: pork, herbs, spring onions, beansprouts, carrot and cooked noodles.

Fill a wide pan with water and soak each wrapper individually until soft; it won't take more than a minute. Take care not to tear them, they will be delicate when soft. (Skip this step if using spring roll wrappers.)

Put a wrapper on a plate and make a 5x2.5cm rectangle of a little of all of the ingredients, placing it about 2.5cm from the end closest to you. Fold the end over it, then fold over the sides, then roll to the end. Take care not to tear it as they will burst when you fry if they have any holes.

Fry either in a shallow pan with about 1cm hot oil, turning to ensure all sides are crispy, or deep-fry until crispy. Drain and serve with the dipping sauce opposite.

I love lentils and think they are much underrated, I often reach for this shepherd's pie recipe over a meaty version as a result. It's a great sharing dish for veggie friends, served in the middle of a table with a big spoon for everyone to help themselves. It's also great for January, when wallets and constitutions are suffering.

Lentil shepherd's pie

Serves 6
For the lentils
1 carrot, quartered and finely chopped
2 celery sticks, finely sliced
1 tbsp light oil
2 garlic cloves, finely chopped
800ml vegetable stock
sprig of thyme
1 bay leaf (optional, but gives lovely fragrance)
250g green or Puy lentils
100g red lentils
sea salt
freshly ground black pepper

For the mash
800g good mashing potatoes such as Maris Piper, peeled
2 tbsp cream or milk (depending on how indulgent you are feeling!)
1 tsp grainy mustard
50g cheese (soft goat's cheese or grated Cheddar both work well)
handful of flat leaf parsley, chopped

Preheat the oven to 180°C/350°F/gas mark 4.
    Sauté the carrot and celery in the oil over a low heat for 10 minutes, until starting to soften. Add the garlic for the final minute.
    Add the stock, thyme, bay leaf, if using, and lentils and bring to a boil. Reduce the heat and simmer for about 20 minutes, until the lentils are tender. Season to taste and leave to the side.
    Boil the potatoes until soft (a knife will go through easily but they won't be too mushy). Mash with the cream or milk. Add the mustard, cheese and parsley and stir through.
    Put the lentils in a deep baking dish (about 20x20cm). Spread the mash on top and decorate with the tines of a fork so that you get ridges which will crisp nicely as it roasts.
    Roast for 15 minutes and serve hot.

I love this dish, especially when made with lovely light and creamy Homemade Paneer (see page 68). It's perfect for healthy veggie days and hot summer lunches. The main ingredients are super-simple, the spices bring out the best in everything. Frozen peas are fine for this but if you can get fresh in-season peas in the pod, even better. Serve with pitta bread, naan bread or rice.

Mutter paneer

Serves 2

For the mutter paneer
1 tbsp coriander seeds
1 tsp cumin seeds
10 peppercorns
2 tbsp light oil
2 shallots, finely chopped
2.5cm fresh root ginger, finely chopped
½ tsp turmeric
1 tsp garam masala
1 red chilli, deseeded and finely chopped
   (keep the seeds in if you're a heat freak)
1 large garlic clove, finely chopped
400g can chopped tomatoes

1 tbsp caster sugar
250g paneer, diced (homemade
   is best, see page 68)
200g frozen peas
sea salt
juice of 1 unwaxed lemon
handful of coriander leaves, chopped

For the salad
8 cherry tomatoes, quartered
handful of coriander leaves, chopped
a little red onion, finely sliced
a little lemon juice (should be enough
   left from the lemon above)

Dry fry the coriander and cumin seeds until fragrant, then grind with the peppercorns in a mortar and pestle.

Heat 1 tbsp of the oil and add the shallots over a gentle heat. Cook until starting to soften. Add the ginger and cook for a minute before adding the freshly ground spices, turmeric, garam masala and chilli. Stir thoroughly and cook for a further few minutes. Stir in the garlic and cook for a minute more. Add the tomatoes and sugar and cook over a low heat for 10 minutes while you work on the paneer.

Fry the paneer in a separate pan in the remaining oil until browning all over. When the paneer is ready, add the peas and 100ml water to the sauce, increase the heat and bring to a boil. Reduce the heat to low and add the paneer.

Cook for a further five minutes. Meanwhile, mix all the ingredients for the salad with a little lemon juice, to taste. Season the mutter paneer with salt and add lemon juice and coriander to taste. Serve immediately.

I have a soft spot for buttermilk. I saw litres of it gracing shop fridges as I grew up in Ireland, where it is used in everyday cooking for soda bread. It is also common in the US, where it is used in pancakes and for fried chicken. If you can't source buttermilk, you can fake it by acidulating 650ml full-fat milk with 100ml natural unsweetened yogurt.

Buttermilk is a perfect marinade, tenderising meat and giving a lovely sourness, similar to yogurt. This recipe makes decadent and delicious chicken nuggets that are impossible to resist. I like to use chicken thigh meat, as it is moist and more flavoursome than breast.

If you don't want to fry you can roast these on an oiled tray for 25–30 minutes at 180°C/350°F/gas mark 4. Turn halfway through cooking to ensure that both sides crisp.

But do fry these if you can, it's important to have an occasional treat!

Buttermilk fried chicken

Serves 6–8 as a snack
750ml buttermilk
2 garlic cloves, coarsely chopped
needles from 2 sprigs of rosemary, finely chopped
600g chicken thigh meat, cut into nugget-sized portions
100g plain flour
sea salt
freshly ground black pepper
2 eggs, beaten
100g breadcrumbs
light oil, to deep-fry (sunflower or groundnut are ideal)

Mix the buttermilk, garlic and rosemary together in a shallow dish. Add the chicken, cover and refrigerate overnight if you can, or for at least four hours. The chicken will benefit immensely from it. Take the chicken from the marinade and let the excess drain off on kitchen paper.

Place the flour in a shallow bowl and season it well. Place the eggs in another bowl and the breadcrumbs in a third. Coat the chicken pieces in the seasoned flour, then in the egg, then the breadcrumbs. If the coating isn't sticking, repeat the egg and breadcrumb part again.

Heat 5cm oil in a very large pan, or a deep fat fryer, until it either reaches 180°C on an oil thermometer, or a piece of bread froths the oil immediately when added. Fry the chicken in batches; don't crowd the pan. Drain on kitchen paper and serve with cocktail sticks.

This is a lively, bolshy salad full of energy and health. It's a slaw really. Raw veg is packed with goodness and – don't tell anyone I told you – but beetroot is detoxifying and good for your liver, so roll this one out for hangovers. The ginger in the dressing is also superb for a sickly tum. Try this salad with Vietnamese Summer Rolls (see page 112).

Carrot and beetroot salad with sesame and orange dressing

Serves 4
For the salad
2 large raw beetroots, peeled and grated
3 carrots, grated
3 spring onions, shredded
1 tbsp sesame seeds

For the dressing
3 tbsp freshly squeezed orange juice
2 tbsp groundnut oil, or other flavourless oil
2.5cm fresh root ginger, finely chopped or grated
sea salt
freshly ground black pepper

Make your dressing by whisking together all the ingredients and seasoning with salt and pepper.

Toss the beetroot, carrot and spring onions just before serving (the beetroot will turn everything pink if you leave it too long), combine with the dressing and serve with the sesame seeds sprinkled on top.

Tomato in béarnaise sounds like it wouldn't work, but the acidity and sweetness is really delicious and it makes a gorgeous dip here. Purple sprouting broccoli is very reasonably priced and, I think, as impressive and flavour-packed as asparagus. It makes great sharing food. People won't have tried this before either, so you will be on to an impressive winner. Try it with Beef, Beet and Horseradish Burgers (see page 121).

Homemade béarnaise is a little tricky but the results are worth it. Aniseedy tarragon adds a lovely edge and roast tomato a fruity layer. This sauce is also great with steak.

Purple sprouting broccoli with tomato and tarragon béarnaise

Serves 4–6
300g purple sprouting broccoli

For the béarnaise
1 large tomato, peeled
1 banana shallot, or 3 normal shallots, finely chopped
100g unsalted butter
50ml white wine vinegar
50ml dry white wine
3 egg yolks
sprig of tarragon, finely chopped
sea salt
freshly ground black pepper

Preheat the oven to 150°C/300°F/gas mark 2. Roast the tomato for 30 minutes until soft. Deseed and chop finely.

Fry the shallots in a little of the butter over a medium heat until soft and transparent, not brown; about five minutes. Add the vinegar and wine and reduce over a medium-high heat until it has halved in volume.

Melt the butter and keep to the side. You will need to use the béarnaise immediately it is ready so, as the butter is melting, steam or roast your purple sprouting broccoli for five minutes, until tender but still firm.

Take the shallot mixture from the heat and slowly whisk in the egg yolks, taking care that they don't split. Slowly add the butter, whisking as you go. Finish with the tarragon and tomato and season to taste.

Sprinkle the broccoli with sea salt and serve with the béarnaise either drizzled over or as a dip on the side.

The earthy beetroot and pungent, spicy horseradish work brilliantly with the minced steak in these burgers. I like the beetroot raw, finely grated it blends with the meat quite well. Cooked will work too. Be warned, this is messy but oh, so satisfying. Your hands will turn bright pink as you mix them. They are best made and cooked immediately; if you let them sit in the moisture from the beetroot, it will make the burgers a little soggy. There is no need to add anything like breadcrumb or egg as some burger recipes do, they only make steak go further if you are trying to spare it and you sacrifice flavour and texture when you do. Try not to overcook them. If you have good minced steak, you should eat them medium rare, when they will have the best flavour and texture. Salt just before you cook too, as salting earlier will result in a loss of moisture and a tough burger. Nobody wants that!

Beef, beet and horseradish burgers

Makes 8
1kg best minced beef (chuck steak works well for this)
2 raw beetroots, peeled and finely grated
5cm fresh horseradish root, finely grated
sea salt

Combine all the ingredients except the salt in a bowl and mix thoroughly with your hands. Divide the mixture into eight equal balls, each about 130g in weight. Shape each into a round and squash down until they are burger shaped.

Cook on a hot griddle or frying pan for three to four minutes on either side, salting only after you turn them over, until still bouncy and moist. Burgers are best served medium rare and, if you have invested in good beef, you will really appreciate it.

Homemade tomato ketchup

Made with good canned tomatoes, this is a pleasure and is actually very quick. I really don't enjoy the processed, over-sweet flavours of most commercially available tomato ketchups and so avoid them. I like my ketchup to be tangy and have some heat, and I like it to have some texture too. I find it's easiest, tastiest and quite cheap to make my own. Ideally we would use in-season fresh tomatoes at their best but, in this part of the world, the season is short and the fruits often expensive. However, if you are making this recipe in the summer, do feel free to substitute the canned tomatoes with 1kg peeled and deseeded fresh lovely tomatoes.

Makes about 1 litre
1 red onion, finely chopped
1 tbsp light oil
2 garlic cloves, finely chopped
1 red chilli, deseeded and finely chopped
2 x 400g cans good sweet tinned tomatoes, such as San Marzano or similar
50g brown sugar
100ml cider vinegar
1 small cinnamon stick
1 bay leaf
sea salt
freshly ground black pepper.

Sauté the onion in the oil over a medium-low heat for about five minutes, until starting to soften. Add the garlic and chilli and cook for a minute. Tip in the tomatoes, sugar, vinegar, cinnamon and bay leaf and bring to a boil. Reduce the heat and cook over a low heat for 45 minutes or so. Remove the bay leaf and cinnamon stick. Season to taste.

I like my ketchup chunky like this but, if you like it smoother, blend and pass through a sieve. This ketchup will keep for a week in the fridge, preferably in an airtight jar.

Lamb shanks, another underrated cut, are available in every Irish supermarket. They're very popular there and I was surprised to see them less available in the UK when I first moved here. That has since changed and now every butcher will have them. They are worth seeking out, as they are a superb cut.

Roasted slowly on the bone, the meat is rich and tender and retains a lot of moisture. I like to marinade shanks in a dry spice rub, here a North African ras el hanout with aromatic dried rose. You can dry your own roses for this (if you haven't put pesticides on them!), or buy them online. It's worth the effort for the lovely quality they impart.

Ras el hanout lamb shanks with couscous

Serves 4

For the ras el hanout
1 tbsp cumin seeds
1 tbsp coriander seeds
1 tbsp black peppercorns
seeds from 8 cardamom pods
2 large cinnamon sticks, broken up
1 tbsp turmeric
10 dried rose buds or 20g dried
    rose petals
1 tbsp sea salt

For the lamb and couscous
4 lamb shanks
4 tbsp light oil
2 carrots, halved lengthways and finely sliced
2 celery sticks, finely sliced
1 onion, finely chopped
2 garlic cloves, finely chopped
400g can good tomatoes
500ml lamb or chicken stock
1 tbsp caster sugar
300g couscous

Make your ras el hanout by first toasting the whole spices in a dry pan over a medium-high heat. Add the turmeric and rose buds and grind in a mortar and pestle or spice grinder with the salt.

Rub the ras el hanout into the lamb shanks, cover and leave for at least two hours in the fridge. Take them out and bring them to room temperature. Preheat the oven to 160°C/325°F/gas mark 3.

Heat the oil in a large ovenproof pan that can hold the shanks – about a three-litre pot – and brown the lamb shanks on all sides. Remove from the pan and put to the side. Fry the carrots, celery and onion over a medium-low heat for eight to 10 minutes until softened. Add the garlic for one minute. Tip in the tomatoes, stock, sugar and lamb. Cover and put in the oven for 2½ hours, until the meat pulls away from the bone.

Leave to rest for 15 minutes. Meanwhile, tip the couscous into a bowl and cover with boiling water. Seal with cling film and, after 10 minutes, fluff it up with a fork. Season and serve with the lamb shanks.

Beef short ribs are relatively uncommon here but are becoming increasingly popular. Much larger than pork ribs, they are also packed with flavour as is anything next to the bone. They are great for barbecues but work really well cooked slowly in the oven. Lots of spices will work here, but I like to use a strong paprika and chilli base to give the illusion of smokiness in oven-baked ribs. Molasses, a deeply savoury, sweet and sticky sugar syrup which is a byproduct of the sugar production process, is super-intense and liquorice-like on its own but, with red wine vinegar to balance, is terrific with beef.

Ask your butcher for the ribs, they will usually be only too delighted to provide them, if they are willing to part with them! Ask them to prepare them and cut them into short ribs. This is another low, slow cook (what else are weekends for?) but you will be rewarded with sweet, smoky, sticky ribs, perfect with buttery mash.

Spiced slow-roast short ribs

Serves 4
1.5kg beef short ribs, trimmed
3 tbsp light oil

For the marinade
60g molasses, or 40g soft dark brown sugar (the sticky one)
80ml red wine vinegar
60ml soy sauce
1 tbsp Worcestershire sauce
4 garlic cloves, chopped
2 tbsp cumin seeds, roasted and ground
2 tbsp mild Spanish paprika
4 tbsp tomato ketchup (homemade is best, see page 122)

Combine all the ingredients for the marinade and massage it into the ribs, in a tray large enough to hold them. Cover and refrigerate for at least two hours, taking them out half an hour before cooking.

Preheat the oven to 150°C/300°F/gas mark 2. Take the ribs out of the marinade and let the excess drip off. Reserve the marinade. Fry the ribs in half the oil in batches, until brown on all sides. Place in a roasting tray oiled with the remaining oil, cover with foil and put in the oven.

After 1½ hours, turn the ribs and brush with the marinade. Cover again and continue to roast for a further 1½ hours. They should be meltingly tender. Remove from the oven and rest for 20 minutes.

Meanwhile, make a sauce by pushing the remaining marinade through a sieve and bringing to a boil, reducing to half its volume over a medium heat. Serve with the short ribs.

Potato dauphinois is a classic creamy dish that I updated slightly and adapted to my taste one day while exploring the contents of my larder. It worked really well, so since then I have made it again and again.

I find sweet potatoes too sweet on their own, so combining them with normal potatoes works perfectly. There isn't as much cream in this dish as you would expect either. This is lovely with a salad or with some simple grilled meat on the side.

Potato and sweet potato dauphinois

Serves 4
2 garlic cloves, finely chopped
1 tsp light oil
75ml double cream
needles from 1 sprig of rosemary, finely chopped
1 bay leaf
250g large waxy potatoes, peeled
250g sweet potatoes, peeled

Preheat the oven to 180°C/350°F/gas mark 4. Sauté the garlic in the oil over a medium heat for 30 seconds, then add the cream, rosemary and bay leaf. Bring to a simmer and turn off the heat. Set aside to allow the herbs and garlic to infuse.

Using a mandolin, finely slice the potatoes into rounds. If you don't have a mandolin use a knife, but do slice as finely as possible.

Take the bay leaf out of the cream and pour the cream over the potatoes. Mix thoroughly with your hands, ensuring that all the slices are coated with cream.

Layer in an ovenproof dish and roast for about 40 minutes; the potatoes will be tender and browning on top. Check for tenderness by piercing the dauphinois with a knife; it should meet no resistance at all until it gets to the bottom of the dish.

Serve warm.

✦ PASSION ✦

Roast bone marrow with a Parmesan crust

Any roast bone marrow dish from me will have to give a nod to Fergus Henderson of St John, the only reason I ever tried it in the first place. Roast bone marrow is a very rich and intensely savoury, umami-packed dish. It is beautiful simply roasted, scooped out of the bone and spread on toast. I also use it as a secret ingredient in beef-based sauces: finely chopped raw bone marrow gives my Gutsy Ragu an extra savoury depth and richness (see page 140).

One bone per person is plenty and it makes a perfect lunch, or even an appetiser (though make sure your main course is lighter). It's so dramatic looking that some of your friends may be taken aback; get them to try it and they will change their minds.

Serves 8
handful of flat leaf parsley, finely chopped
50g dried breadcrumbs
50g finely grated Parmesan
sea salt
8 bone marrow shafts, halved vertically or horizontally
(whatever your butcher can provide), with extra meat on
the bone removed (your butcher can do this)

Preheat the oven to 180°C/350°F/gas mark 4. Combine the parsley, breadcrumbs and Parmesan and season with a little salt.

Place the bones in a roasting tray with the largest bone marrow surface facing up. Cover the exposed bone marrow with the breadcrumb mixture. Roast for 15–20 minutes, until the marrow is starting to soften and is buttery in texture.

Serve spread on good sourdough toast with some of that lovely crust mixed in.

Lamb breast is a very cheap cut, it's basically the belly of the lamb or ribs. Many butchers throw it away as it's not worth the effort to get the meat off the bones for the mincer and, as it is quite fatty, it has fallen out of favour in our fat-obsessed times. It is silliness really, fat – in moderation – is not bad for you. And it is where the flavour lies.

Lamb breast with persillade crust

Serves 6
2 tbsp light oil
2 lamb breasts, trimmed, with
    a layer of fat remaining on top
2 handfuls flat leaf parsley, chopped
6 garlic cloves, finely chopped
100g breadcrumbs
1 tbsp sea salt

Preheat your oven to 200°C/400°F/gas mark 6.
    Oil two baking trays that will fit the lamb breasts and place one breast in each tray, fat side up.
    Combine the parsley, garlic, breadcrumbs and salt and spread liberally over the top.
    Roast for 20 minutes. Remove from the oven and cover with foil. Reduce the oven temperature to 180°C/350°F/gas mark 4. Roast for a further 1½ hours.
    Leave to rest for 10 minutes before serving. The lamb is quite rich so this goes really well with some salad.

✦ PASSION ✦

Slow-cooked pork cheeks in cider

Pork cheeks are super-cheap and delicious. A traditional cut in Ireland and the UK, they fell out of favour some years ago but are sneaking their way back in. My mother used to tell us – to frighten us into eating our stew – that she and her sisters fought over the cheeks on the pig's head they had for dinner, as it is the best bit. It really is.

Full-flavoured and rich, cheeks benefit from a long, slow cook and are lovely braised, darker than other cuts. Like anything that takes time, it is worth making extra. Leftovers are especially good as a pie filling; think cold winter's evenings and solace.

Pig's cheeks are becoming increasingly easy to source, some supermarkets stock them and you can also ask your butcher to reserve some for you.

Serves 4–6
5 shallots or 2 onions, finely chopped
2 tbsp light oil
3 garlic cloves, finely chopped
1kg pork cheeks, trimmed by your butcher
500ml dry cider
1 tbsp Dijon mustard
750ml chicken or pork stock
2 bay leaves
handful of flat leaf parsley, chopped

Sauté the onions in half the oil over a medium heat for about five minutes, until they start to soften without going brown. Add the garlic and sauté for a minute or so.

In a separate pan, brown the pork cheeks in the remaining oil in batches, taking care not to crowd the pan otherwise they will stew.

Add the pork to the garlic and onion and deglaze the pork pan with a little of the cider, to mop up all of those lovely porky bits. Add to the pork with the rest of the cider, bring to a boil and reduce the cider by about one-third. Add the mustard, stock and bay leaves, reduce the heat, cover and cook gently over a low heat on the hob for 2½ hours, stirring occasionally. (Alternatively, cook, covered, in an oven preheated to 150°C/300°F/gas mark 2 for the same time.)

Check that the pork is fork-tender and pulls away at the slightest touch; that's when it is done. Take from the heat and stir in the parsley. Serve hot.

Eight Great Big Dinners...

...and what to do with the leftovers

I love cooking for a crowd and find big joints of meat dramatic, delicious and a joy to tuck into. Far more often than that though, I cook a joint for only a small group of friends – sometimes just for me – which presents me with the joy of leftovers. Far from being an annoyance, most things taste better the next day and are great to cook with and to eat. Some good pastry transforms the humble leftover into a wonderful pie. Dumpling wrappers with leftover roast meat make superb dumplings that can be dropped in a soup made from the leftover bones.

And it's not only meat that keeps on giving. I present you with the humble spud: leftovers sliced and fried become delicious, crispy sautéed potatoes; mashed and combined with fish and herbs, a gorgeous fish cake. These days, I deliberately cook extra to save time and make life easier.

I often roast large pumpkins and squash, in fact once I roasted a specimen that was two feet high! Although that was an unusual gift from a local allotment, delivered in segments in a cement bag, I do roast large squashes in segments so I can use the pumpkin over the following days or freeze to use later. It makes life more efficient and sweeter.

One of my regular weekend chores is batch cooking lots of beans. Why? They taste better than canned, they're super-cheap and, after I freeze them in 300g amounts, they're available for stews, soups, bean mashes, or anything for weeks to follow.

This chapter includes some of my very favourite ways of BIG cooking. I encourage you to adopt the habit. Far from making your life more difficult, it will simplify it, make eating well far cheaper and your food tastier.

When I had my stall at Covent Garden I wanted the tastiest, most luscious lamb for my homemade bread roll sandwiches, but I needed to sleep to survive my crazy 17-hour days. So I developed this overnight lamb recipe, which greeted me with wafts of deliciousness as I made my way down the stairs ready to start a day's work. You can, of course, cook it in the morning for dinner that night.

Cinnamon is wonderful with lamb, reminiscent of autumn evenings or summer barbecues. It may seem OTT to grind your own, but you'll be rewarded tenfold in flavour.

This will feed many more in sandwiches or picnic wraps. I serve it with my Smoky Aubergine Relish (see page 134), but anything tomato-based will work really well.

When thinking leftovers, remember lamb loves mint, coriander, sumac, cumin, aubergine and tomato, so feel free to play around with these flavours. The leftover lamb is tender and rich and works well in many different places. My favourites follow this recipe.

Overnight shoulder of lamb

Serves 4–6
2 tbsp cumin seeds
4 cinnamon sticks, or 1½ tbsp ground cinnamon
2 red chillies, deseeded and finely chopped
4 garlic cloves, finely chopped
5cm fresh root ginger, finely chopped
sea salt
a little oil, sunflower or olive will do fine
1 x 2.5kg whole shoulder of lamb
6 tomatoes, halved

Toast the cumin seeds over a high heat in a dry pan. Grind with a mortar and pestle (or spice or coffee grinder) with the cinnamon to a powder. Add the chilli, garlic and ginger and grind some more. Add salt to taste and enough oil to make a paste, then rub it all over the lamb. Cover and marinate in the fridge for as long as you can; a minimum of two hours.

When you're ready to cook, bring the lamb to room temperature. Preheat the oven to 220°C/425°F/gas mark 7. Place the lamb in a deep roasting tray and roast for 20 minutes. Remove from the oven and reduce the temperature to 100°C/212°F/gas mark ¼. Add the tomatoes to the roasting tin, cover with foil and place in the oven for 8¾ hours, while you sleep or get on with your day!

The lamb will be creamily tender with lovely seasoned skin. Rest for 30 minutes before eating with the sticky, almost date-like tomatoes.

Tip: while your oven is on for a long time at a low temperature, it's the perfect opportunity to slow-roast vegetables if you have room.

Pairing lamb and aubergine again, I know, but they are so good together. This is like a Middle Eastern caponata, the Italian aubergine stew, with some lamb in!

Lamb and aubergine stew

Serves 4
1 tbsp cumin seeds
1 red onion, finely chopped
1 small aubergine, chopped
2 tbsp olive oil
2 garlic cloves, finely chopped
1 red chilli, deseeded and finely chopped
500g leftover lamb shoulder, in large chunks
400g can good chopped tomatoes
1 tbsp sumac
sea salt
freshly ground black pepper
handful of coriander leaves, chopped

Toast the cumin seeds over a high heat in a dry pan. Grind with a mortar and pestle (or spice or coffee grinder) to a powder.

Sauté the onion and aubergine in the oil over a medium-low heat until starting to soften. Add the cumin, garlic and chilli.

Tip in the lamb, tomatoes and sumac. Bring to just before a boil and allow to simmer gently for 20 minutes.

Season to taste and finish with the coriander leaves. Serve with toasted bread, couscous or rice.

This is a gorgeous, rustic and flavoursome use of leftover lamb shoulder. It also costs just pennies and is ridiculously simple. Serve with the smoky aubergine relish.

Lamb and potato cakes

Serves 4 for a snack, or 2 for supper
For the smoky aubergine relish
2 aubergines
4 roast tomatoes (roasted with the lamb
    shoulder, if you have any left)
2 tbsp tahini
1 tbsp pomegranate molasses
1 tbsp sumac
1 tbsp cumin, toasted and ground
1 red chilli, deseeded and chopped
handful of coriander leaves, chopped

For the potato cakes
500g potatoes, peeled
sea salt
25g unsalted butter
350g leftover lamb shoulder, shredded
3 spring onions, finely chopped
50g plain flour, plus more to dust
handful of flat leaf parsley, chopped
freshly ground black pepper
2 tbsp light oil

To make the relish, burn the aubergines all round over a gas flame until black and squishy. Allow to cool and peel the skin off. Don't worry if you can't get it all off. Mash the flesh. Combine with the other ingredients except the coriander and roughly blend, leaving in some chunks.

Put the potatoes in a large pan of salted water, bring to a boil and simmer for 15 minutes, or until tender to the point of a knife. Drain well and mash. Melt the butter in a small saucepan. In a large bowl, combine the lamb, mashed potatoes, butter, spring onions, flour, parsley and seasoning. Flour your hands, and collect a handful of the mixture. Shape into a ball and flatten. Repeat until all the mixture has been used.

Heat the oil in a large frying pan over a medium heat. When hot, add the potato cakes, making sure not to crowd the pan (you may have to fry in batches). Cook for three to four minutes on either side until browned.

Stir the coriander through the relish and serve with the potato cakes.

Samosas are terrific comfort food. Samosa wrappers are available from Asian food shops and most supermarkets, but it's easier to find filo pastry, which is what I use here. These are very quick to make and, once you have got the hang of rolling them into triangular packages, they take just seconds to assemble. Once rolled they also freeze very well, each wrapped individually in greaseproof paper. That's just in case you can't face eating lamb five days running...

Spiced lamb samosas

Serves 4
1 tbsp cumin seeds
½ onion, finely chopped
1 tbsp light oil
500g leftover lamb shoulder, chopped
150 frozen peas, defrosted
250g filo pastry
50g unsalted butter, melted, or 150ml olive oil
light oil, to deep-fry (optional)

Toast the cumin seeds over a high heat in a dry pan. Grind with a mortar and pestle (or spice or coffee grinder) to a powder.

Fry the onion in the oil with the cumin until soft. Tip into a bowl and add the lamb and peas. Combine well, using your hands.

Cut the filo pastry into rectangles, each about 20x10cm. Lay them out and brush liberally with butter or oil. Put 1 tbsp of the meat filling about 5cm in from one end of the pastry.

Fold the pastry edge over the filling to form a triangle, then roll to the end, keeping the triangle shape. Repeat to use up the lamb.

Samosas are best deep-fried. Heat 5cm oil, if using, in a very large pan, or a deep fat fryer, until it reaches 180°C on an oil thermometer, or a piece of bread froths the oil immediately when added. Fry the samosas in batches until golden, drain on kitchen paper and serve warm.

They are good cooked in the oven too, if you prefer; bake in a preheated oven at 180°C/350°F/gas mark 4 for about 25 minutes.

I love these and used to sell them at my market stall. Use shop-bought pastry (puff or shortcrust) if you wish, but I love to use homemade butter-rich shortcrust. I like to make big chunky rolls that would satisfy for a whole meal. They make terrific picnic lunches.

Lamb and smoky aubergine rolls

Makes 4 chunky sausage rolls
For the shortcrust pastry
150g plain flour, plus more to dust
sea salt
75g unsalted butter, chilled and diced
1 egg, beaten

For the filling
1 large aubergine
2 garlic cloves, finely chopped
1 tbsp olive oil
500g leftover lamb shoulder, chopped
1 heaped tbsp sumac
handful of coriander leaves, chopped
freshly ground black pepper
1 egg, beaten

First make the pastry: sift the flour with a little salt and add the butter. Rub quickly with your fingers until it looks like breadcrumbs. Add the egg and bring together with a knife (to keep it cool). Add a little water if needed. Shape into a ball, wrap in cling film and refrigerate for an hour.

Blacken the aubergine over a gas flame, rotating until it looks like there is no hope... that's when it's perfect! Let cool. Preheat the oven to 200°C/400°F/gas mark 6. Sauté the garlic in the oil for a minute. Place the lamb and sumac in a bowl and tip in the garlic. Peel and chop the aubergine (don't worry about little bits of skin that stubbornly remain). Add to the lamb with the coriander. Season to taste.

Roll the pastry out on a floured surface to 5mm thick; you want it to be sturdy. Cut into rectangles about 15x12.5cm. Place the lamb mixture in a line about 2.5cm in from one edge. Brush both edges with beaten egg, fold over the pastry and press. I also fold the pastry back towards the filling (see photo opposite) to ensure it is well sealed.

Prick holes with a fork or slash at intervals with a knife. Brush once more with beaten egg to ensure the rolls turn nice and brown. Cut into 10cm rolls. Bake for 25–30 minutes until crisp. Serve hot or cold.

Spiced beef is a grand Cork Christmas tradition. I grew up nearby and we didn't have it locally at all, but my mother is from Cork and so I learned about it pretty quickly. Brisket or topside is cured and spiced over a week or more, depending on the recipe. Different butchers have different recipes, but the spice flavour always smacks of Christmas. It has really interesting origins... traders from Asia would travel to Cork's Butter Market – at the time the largest in Europe – and trade spices for butter. In Ireland we never made spiced beef, but bought it. This wasn't possible in London though, so I figured out quickly how to make it. You'll need to start the cure a good week before cooking the beef.

Saltpetre, a preservative, can be difficult to find now as it is also used to make explosives(!), but you can source it online. Your butcher may give you some, too.

Spiced beef

Serves 8
2kg beef brisket, off the bone

For the curing mix
1 tsp allspice
1 tsp cloves
1 tsp freshly grated nutmeg
1 tsp mace
75g soft brown sugar
10g saltpetre
100g sea salt

Combine all the ingredients for the curing mix and rub it all over the brisket. Sterilise a non-metallic pot or plastic container into which the beef will fit snugly with boiling water. Add the beef, cover and store in the fridge for eight days, turning daily and basting with any juices.

Wipe off the excess marinade and cover the beef with water in a large saucepan. Bring to a boil and simmer gently for two hours.

Allow to cool and serve over the festive period thinly sliced, as you would a ham.

✦ LEFTOVERS ✦

Spiced beef toastie

This is simple and a bit of a guilty pleasure.

Slice spiced beef and a decent strong cheese such as Cheddar. This makes a lovely Christmas snack, on toast, or in a toasted sandwich.

Spiced beef hash

The ultimate Christmas brunch.

Leftover potatoes fried with chunks of spiced beef and served with chopped flat leaf parsley and a soft-fried egg will sooth any manner of over-indulgence … and prepare you for the next lot.

Spiced beef mini pasties

Another great Christmas snack.

Tuck spiced beef with grated cheese in some folded shop-bought puff pastry. Brush with beaten egg and bake for 10–15 minutes at 200°C/400°F/gas mark 6 until crisp.

✦ PASSION ✦

Gutsy ragu with gremolata

I am convinced that there are more opinions on ragu than on anything else in the world. Depending on who you talk to you're told never white wine, always red wine. Never use milk. It's a minefield. Whenever in doubt when it comes to Italian food I refer to Marcella Hazan, and Marcella says milk and white wine, so I tried that. And I liked it. The milk sweetens and the wine adds acidity, and that works for me. Always cook with a wine you would drink as, if you don't like the wine, you won't like your ragu.

Serves 6

For the ragu and pasta
3 carrots, quartered lengthways and finely sliced
3 celery sticks, finely sliced
2 tbsp light olive oil
3 garlic cloves, finely chopped
1kg beef shin on the bone, meat removed and finely chopped or minced
50g bone marrow, scooped from the beef shin bone, finely chopped
400ml white wine
400ml full-fat milk
3 bay leaves
2 x 400g cans good tomatoes
sea salt
freshly ground black pepper
750g pappardelle

For the gremolata
handful of flat leaf parsley, chopped
4 garlic cloves, finely chopped
finely grated zest of 1 unwaxed lemon

Saute the carrots and celery on a medium-low heat for eight to 10 minutes until softening. Add the garlic for a minute or so. Add the meat and bone marrow and brown with the vegetables. When browned, pour in the wine and boil off the alcohol over about two or three minutes. Add the milk and bay leaves, bring to a simmer, reduce the heat and cook gently for three hours, stirring occasionally so it doesn't stick. Add the tomatoes when most of the liquid has evaporated. Season to taste. Cook the pappardelle according to packet instructions. Combine the ingredients for the gremolata. Toss the ragu with the pappardelle. Serve with the gremolata on top.

Ragu and potato rolls

Follow the recipe for Lamb and Smoky Aubergine Rolls (see page 136), only substitute 300g cooked potato, a handful of flat leaf parsley and 400g ragu, roughly mashed together, as filling. Roll as instructed and brush with a beaten egg to ensure they go nice and brown when baked. Makes 4.

Ragu and potato cakes

Combine 250g of leftover ragu with 500g mashed potatoes, 50g plain flour, 2 shredded spring onions, a handful of chopped flat leaf parsley and seasoning. Shape into balls and dip in seasoned flour, then in egg and finally in breadcrumbs. Deep-fry until brown and crispy and serve on cocktail sticks as nibbles. Serves 4 as part of a spread.

Mini ragu pies

This doesn't require much instruction, or indeed any amounts. Preheat the oven to 180°C/350°F/gas mark 4. Simply place leftover ragu in buttered or oiled small pie dishes and cover with a puff pastry lid. Brush the lid with beaten egg and bake for 20 minutes or so, until crisp.

Ragu and potato bake

Peel and finely slice 1kg potatoes with a mandolin. Add 75ml double cream and mix with your hands to ensure that all slices are coated. Put three layers of potatoes in a buttered ovenproof dish, add a layer of ragu and repeat until you have used all the potatoes, finishing with a layer of potatoes on top. Grate some Gruyère on top to finish and bake at 180°C/350°F/gas mark 4 for 30 minutes until brown and crispy. Serves 4 with a green salad on the side.

People often throw away leftover pasta. I never do. It is delicious fried up the next day. That may sound wrong, but it really works. The Italians do it too, so it's worth a try, isn't it?

Ragu and pappardelle omelette

Serves 2
leftover pappardelle and ragu, as much as you have
2 eggs
handful of flat leaf parsley, chopped
sea salt
freshly ground black pepper
1 tbsp light oil

Combine all the ingredients except the oil and season with salt and pepper. Fry in the oil in a hot pan for 2–3 minutes, then put a plate on top, slide the omelette on to it and flip it to cook on the other side. (Alternatively finish it under the grill for a couple of minutes until brown.) Serve in slices, as you would a tortilla, with some salad.

Empanadas are a lovely savoury snack found all over South America. They are like a dumpling that has been wrapped with a heavier dough, so they are sturdier and crisper. Like a mini pastie, really.

They are a perfect way to use up leftover ragu, especially if you don't have a lot left. Proper South American empanadas use a specific dough, but I find that simple pizza dough works very well here. Indeed, it's a perfect use for leftover pizza dough, which freezes very well. If you have any leftover, simply roll it out, and freeze pizza – or empanada – sized sheets layered between greaseproof paper. So, all those scraps of dough that you used to throw away? Don't, you never know when you can use them.

Ragu empanadas are rich, deeply savoury and delicious. Play around with the fillings: squash, spinach, chilli and goat's cheese is a fantastic vegetarian version. Shredded chilli chicken is a nice light meat filling. Any meaty leftovers with sauce, shredded (such as Spiced Slow-roast Short Ribs, see page 124, or Slow-cooked Pork Cheeks in Cider, see page 129) make a great empanada stuffing.

This recipe is just a guide, which is why there are no amounts; it's all about how much ragu you have leftover. So make as many as you can and enjoy them. These are great lunch fodder too, so don't be afraid to stick some in your lunchbox. Traditionally these are fried, as I do here. If you would prefer a healthier version, bake them in an oven preheated to 200°C/400°F/gas mark 6 for 12–15 minutes. Brush them with beaten egg if baking, so they turn a nice golden brown.

Ragu empanadas

leftover Pizza Dough, or make some fresh (see page 98)
leftover ragu, as much as you have
flat leaf parsley
light oil, to fry

Roll your dough into thin 15cm circles.

Put a couple of tablespoons of ragu filling, plus some parsley, into the centre, brush the edges with water and fold the dough over, creating a half-moon shape. Press the edges together then crimp them with a fork, ensuring they are tightly shut.

Heat about 1cm of oil in a pan until a cube of bread froths the oil immediately when added. Fry the empanadas for two to three minutes on each side. Serve hot or cold. These are a perfect picnic snack.

✦ PASSION ✦

Overnight shoulder of pork with spiced apple relish

This is a great weekend roast and special occasion dish and I've made it for Christmas, which gifted me a stress-free Christmas Day. The pork chugged away nicely on its own and left me with only a small amount to do on the day itself. A 12-hour roast results in meltingly tender pork you can pull apart with your fingers and sensational crackling. I add cider vinegar to the relish as I find its sharpness great with rich pork. It's sublime in a sandwich (with the meat and crackling) in a fluffy Irish blaa (see page 88). When thinking leftovers, think fennel, sage, lemon, beans, cabbage and mustard.

Serves 8
3.5–4kg bone-in shoulder of pork, skin scored by your butcher
sea salt

For the spiced apple sauce
6 Bramley apples
50ml cider vinegar
50g caster sugar
1 nutmeg
2 cinnamon sticks, broken up
1 red chilli, chopped

Preheat the oven to 220°C/425°F/gas mark 7. Boil a kettle and place the pork on a wire rack, skin side up, in the sink. Pour boiling water over the skin and drain. This puffs up the skin so it's ready to crackle. Wipe the skin bone dry with kitchen paper. Salt it with coarse sea salt. Roast for 20 minutes, cover with foil and reduce the oven temperature to 120°C/250°F/gas mark ½. Roast for 11 hours. Remove the foil, return the heat to 220°C/425°F/gas mark 7 and roast for 10-15 minutes. You should have perfect crackling. Ensure you don't burn it at this stage and ruin all your hard work! Rest for at least 15 minutes. The pork will be so tender you can serve it with a spoon.

Meanwhile, peel and core the apples and boil with 50ml water, the vinegar, sugar and spices until the apples are mushy. Serve with the spices still in.

Tip: the pork fat rendered out in the slow roasting process is terrific with roast spuds. Even better than goose fat, I say. Save it in a bowl or jar in your fridge.

I love this dish, shreds of pork mingling with – preferably – home-cooked black beans (see page 160) and tomato is a delicious evening meal. It's great with rice, but I prefer to eat it with some toasted good bread.

Pork and black bean chilli

Serves 2
1 tbsp cumin seeds
1 red onion, finely chopped
1 red chilli, deseeded and finely chopped
1 tbsp olive oil
1 garlic clove, finely chopped
400g leftover pork shoulder, chopped
300g black beans (home-cooked are best, see page 160), or
    400g can black beans, drained and rinsed
1 tbsp brown sugar
400g can tomatoes
handful of coriander leaves, chopped

Toast the cumin seeds over a high heat in a dry pan. Grind with a mortar and pestle (or spice or coffee grinder) to a powder.

Sauté the onion and chilli in the oil until soft. Add the garlic for the last minute.

Add the cumin, pork, the beans if home-cooked, brown sugar and tomatoes. Bring to a boil, reduce the heat and simmer for 20 minutes. Add the beans, if canned, for the last five minutes.

Finish with the coriander and it's ready to eat.

Pork croquettes

Croquettes are lovely as a meal in themselves – think light lunch – but also great as a side to a big meal. The leftover pork will be really moist so won't need much assistance in sticking together.

Preheat the oven to 200°C/400°F/gas mark 6. Season 500g of leftover pork shoulder, chopped. If it's a little dry (and it really shouldn't be), add a beaten egg, or as much of it as is needed to function as a glue. Shape into cylinders about 7.5cm long and coat in seasoned flour, then beaten egg and finally breadcrumbs. Bake for 20 minutes, or deep-fry until crispy. Serves 2.

Pork and potato cakes with kale and an egg

How to improve the humble potato cake? Put pork in it! Delicious and cheap, it's a perfect speedy supper.

Mash 500g boiled potatoes, add 20g unsalted butter, 25g plain flour, a handful of flat leaf parsley, chopped and 300g leftover pork shoulder, shredded. Season to taste. If your potatoes were very fluffy you may need to add a beaten egg to hold the mixture together: try and form a patty and, if it won't hold, you will know you need to add one.

Fry the cakes in 1 tbsp light oil over a medium heat for about five minutes on each side until warmed through. Serve with some lightly pan-fried kale or cavolo nero and a fried or poached egg. Be sure to keep that lovely yolk soft and allow it to dribble over the cake when you pierce it with your knife. Serves 4 as a starter or 2 as supper.

✦ PASSION ✦

Two- and six-hour pork belly

My obsession with pork belly became infamous in the early days of my blog. I am quite faddish with food anyway, developing love affairs with favourite ingredients before I overdose and need a break. I could write about The Pork Chronicles, The Chorizo Files and a brief affair with dill from which I have never recovered. Pork belly has remained a keeper though. Who can resist that gorgeous rich flesh with its crackling cap? I can't.

Your choices here are determined by time. When I am hungry and impatient, I reach for the two-hour dish. When I have time, I love to let pork belly roast slowly; ideal for Sunday lunch when you put it in first thing. The cider-braised lentils are perfect with it.

Serves 4
2kg pork belly joint, skin scored by the butcher
sea salt
2 carrots, quartered lengthways and sliced
1 celery stick, finely sliced
1 shallot, finely chopped
1 tbsp light oil
300g Puy lentils
2 bay leaves
350ml dry cider
350ml light stock, such as chicken or pork

Preheat the oven to 230°C/450°F/gas mark 8. Ensure your meat is at room temperature. Put the pork on a wire rack in your sink and pour boiling water over it. This puffs the skin and is one secret to good crackling. Dry the meat and skin thoroughly with kitchen paper. Just before you put it in the oven, and not a minute before, salt liberally with sea salt, rubbing it all over the joint. (If you do this too early it will ruin your crackling.) Put the pork in the oven for 15 minutes.

Reduce the oven temperature to 170°C/340°F/gas mark 3½ and roast for 1½ hours, for two-hour pork, or to 120°C/250°F/gas mark ½ for 5½ hours for the six-hour version. Meanwhile, sauté the carrots, celery and shallot in the oil for six to eight minutes. Take off the heat and mix with the lentils and bay leaves. Add to the pork with the cider and stock when the two-hour pork has 30 minutes left, or the six-hour pork has 1½ hours left. In both cases, return the oven to 230°C/450°F/gas mark 8 for a final 15 minutes to crisp the crackling, keeping an eye on it to ensure it doesn't burn.

Make dumpling wrappers (see page 56) or buy shop-bought wonton skins or dumpling wrappers from Asian stores or large supermarkets.

Pork belly dumplings in broth

Serves 4
For the broth
pork or chicken bones, or chicken carcasses
2 tbsp light oil
2 carrots, peeled and chopped
1 leek, washed and chopped
2–3 garlic cloves, whole, plus 2 more, finely chopped
small handful of black peppercorns
2.5cm fresh root ginger, finely chopped
1 mild green chilli, finely chopped

For the dumplings
sea salt
freshly ground black pepper
500g leftover pork belly, shredded
150g Chinese cabbage or other greens, shredded
20 dumpling wrappers
a few Chinese chives, chopped
3–4 spring onions, shredded

To make the broth, fry the bones in half the oil until caramelised, then place in a pot with the carrots, leek, whole garlic and peppercorns. Cover with water and bring to a boil, scooping off any scum. Simmer for a couple of hours. Strain the broth and keep to the side.

Make the dumplings by putting 1 tsp of seasoned leftover pork belly and some shredded greens into a dumpling wrapper. Rub the edges with water and press closed. Make about six dumplings per person.

Sauté the ginger, green chilli and chopped garlic in the remaining oil for a minute or two. Add the broth and bring to a boil. Reduce the heat and add the dumplings. Cook for three or four minutes, no longer or they may burst.

Serve the broth and dumplings in bowls, sprinkling each with some Chinese chives and spring onions.

Pork belly pancakes

I like to make this simple quick twist on Chinese duck pancakes. You will need to take a trip to the local Asian food shop for the pancakes.

Steam the pancakes in a bamboo steamer or in a foil parcel in your oven for 10 minutes, or according to the packet instructions. Stuff them with shredded warmed leftover pork belly, shredded cucumber and spring onions and hoisin sauce. Scale the amounts up or down depending on how much leftover meat you have and how many mouths there are to feed. Serve as a snack or a hearty starter.

Pork, cavolo nero and noodle soup

Make a broth as for the Pork Belly Dumplings in Broth (see opposite), adding the ginger, garlic and chill, then similar amounts of leftover pork belly, shredded cavolo nero or kale and a handful of egg or rice noodles. Cook for as long as the noodles require, season and serve warm. Serves 4.

Crackling tips

No, this isn't leftovers, but I did tell you I was passionate about roast pork. This information is vital for fellow crackling lovers, and I had to fit it in somewhere!

Dry skin! Whether through wiping with kitchen paper or using a hair dryer (I don't believe this is necessary, but some people swear by it)
Puff up the skin with boiling water to start the crackling off.
Salt just before you put it in the oven.
Only put dry spices and salt on the skin. Wet rubs will result in soggy skin.
Keep the heat high at the beginning and the end of cooking, watching as you go.

And a cheat. If you are still unhappy with your crackling – and you really shouldn't be, but just in case! – you can always crisp it under the grill. But do take care as it is extremely easy to ruin all your good work and burn it at this stage.

One chicken can go a very long way. Roast it and feast on the leftovers for a couple of days, or joint it for several meals. Jointing a chicken is easy and soon you'll be able to do it in minutes. Don't waste anything, everything from the skin to the carcass is delicious.

A perfect roast chicken requires a few things, it needs to be moist and flavoursome and it needs to be crispy. The first place to start is with a good chicken, free-range organic are best, although free-range is the most important part.

Perfect roast chicken

Serves 4
1 chicken (about 1kg)
1 unwaxed lemon, halved
a few sprigs of thyme
4 garlic cloves
50g unsalted butter
sea salt

Preheat the oven to 200°C/400°F/gas mark 6. Remove the thick layer of fat from inside the chicken. This fat – known as shmaltz – is highly prized in Jewish cooking; save it for a batch of potatoes, it's delicious!

Put the lemon, thyme and garlic in the cavity. Rub the butter into the skin generously, smothering it, and sprinkle over some sea salt.

Roast for 20 minutes, breast up. Reduce the oven temperature to 180°C/350°F/gas mark 4. Turn the chicken breast down and roast for 25 minutes. Turn breast up again and roast for 25 minutes more.

Check the chicken is cooked by pulling the leg away from the body; the juices should run clear. Continue to cook if you see any trace of pink.

Rest for 10 minutes for the juices to settle. Now it's ready to serve.

How to joint a chicken

A pair of poultry shears is a wise investment. Pull the legs away from the body. Cut around the leg then pull it from the body, releasing the joint from the socket by twisting. Split the leg and thigh by feeling for the space in the bone and cutting it with your shears.

Remove the wings by twisting at the joint and cutting to remove. Remove the breast meat by cutting away from you with a slim, flexible knife as close as you can to the carcass. Save the carcass for stock.

Peel off any extra skin and store it for skewers (see page 154).

Take the fat from inside the chicken and save for roast potatoes.

This is a lovely, rustic, flavour-packed dish perfect for all year round; it's spritely in summer and comforting in winter. It also makes the best of the delicious chicken legs and thighs, which taste so much better than the breast. They are also way cheaper. Cooking chorizo is best here but dried is fine too, just don't buy the sliced stuff!

Roast chicken legs and thighs with tomato and chorizo

Serves 2
250g chorizo
1 tbsp light oil
2 garlic cloves, finely chopped
400g can chopped tomatoes
1 tbsp brown sugar
1 tbsp olive oil
2 chicken thighs
2 chicken legs
sea salt
handful of flat leaf parsley, chopped

Preheat your oven to 180°C/350°F/gas mark 4.

Start the sauce by sautéing the chorizo in the light oil for four to five minutes over a medium heat, until it has released its oils and is starting to crisp. Add the garlic for one minute. Tip in the tomatoes and sugar, reduce the heat and cook for 10 minutes.

Place the tomato and chorizo sauce in an ovenproof dish that will fit the chicken. Rub the olive oil into the chicken skin, sprinkle it with salt, and place skin side up on the sauce.

Roast for 40 minutes. Check that the chicken is crisped and cooked through. It's ready when it is.

Sprinkle with the parsley and serve.

I love these, they are a real guilty pleasure and I eat them far too often. Chicken skin is such a treasure, I can't believe people throw it away! Years ago, when I was in Japan, I encountered one of the single best dishes I have ever eaten: a dish of gyoza dumplings wrapped in chicken skin, deep-fried and served with thick, sweet Japanese mayonnaise. This was just one eating house among a throng of small, fantastic chicken grill places, hidden down alleys, where the American GIs once hung out after World War 2. Different parts of the chicken are grilled on skewers over coals: innards, skin, thigh... anything. I recreate these with chicken skin here. There aren't any amounts in this recipe, as it depends on how much chicken skin you can get your hands on!

Chicken skin skewers

wooden skewers
pinch of Chinese five spice
pinch of chilli flakes
sea salt
chicken skin

Preheat your oven to 180°C/350°F/gas mark 4. Soak the skewers in cold water for 20 minutes.

Rub the five spice, chilli and a little salt into the chicken skin. Wrap around the skewers and suspend the skewers over two opposite sides of an ovenproof dish, so none of the chicken skin is touching the dish.

Roast for 10 minutes until crispy.

Who says it is expensive to eat well? This is the perfect use for leftover roast chicken. A carcass will contribute to a delicious fresh chicken stock and shredded leftover meat goes into the soup. It's also possible to make this with raw chicken meat, preferably thigh as it tastes much better and retains its moisture, although as it is a soup breast meat will do fine, too.

This soup is wonderfully aromatic with lovely lemon grass, coriander and ginger to lift the soul. A little chilli heat and some garlic complete the set. Thick rice noodles are my preference for this, although any noodles that you've got will do. You can even break up thin pasta and add it to the broth.

This recipe makes two big bowls for a filling supper. I would never want to eat this soup any other way.

Aromatic chicken noodle soup

Serves 2

2 lemon grass stalks, trimmed, halved lengthways
    and finely chopped
1 red chilli, deseeded and finely chopped
2.5cm fresh root ginger, finely chopped
1 tbsp light oil
2 garlic cloves, finely chopped
300g leftover chicken, shredded, or raw and sliced
800ml best chicken stock (homemade from the chicken
    carcass is best, see page 150)
150g thick rice noodles, or egg noodles
sea salt
freshly ground black pepper
½ unwaxed lemon
handful of coriander leaves

Fry the lemon grass, chilli and ginger in the oil for a couple of minutes over a medium to high heat. Add the garlic and cook for 30 seconds.

Add the chicken and, if raw, fry until cooked on the outside (a couple of minutes). If cooked, just mix with the other ingredients.

Add the stock and cook for five minutes to let the flavours develop, then add the noodles and cook according to the packet instructions (it should take no more than a few minutes).

Season and serve with a squeeze of lemon, scattered with coriander.

Pumpkins and squashes are wonderful ingredients. Sweet in flavour, they go really well with intensely savoury ingredients such as pancetta or ham. Soft, they love crispy things such as fried sage; gentle, they go well with strong aromas such as lemon grass. There are many varieties, shapes and sizes. You can stuff and roast tiny squashes. I love to roast great big ones in wedges and do lots of different things with the resulting purée. Why roast? The roasting intensifies the flavour as the pumpkin loses water and you are left with a tastier and more manageable ingredient.

How to roast a pumpkin

First, tackle the pumpkin and cut it into more manageable chunks. It's easier to leave the skin on and worry about that later. You do need to take the seeds out though, which is very easy. Cut the pumpkin in half and scoop the seeds out with a spoon. (You can eat the seeds too, they're delicious roasted and salted once you have removed them from the stringy flesh.) I usually cut large round pumpkins into six or eight wedges, and long squashes like butternut into two.

To roast, place the wedges skin side down on an oiled tray and roast in a preheated oven at 180°C/350°F/gas mark 4 until soft.

Use immediately as a side dish with spiced olive oil, or peel and store any extra in the fridge for three days, or in the freezer.

What to do with your roasted pumpkin? Read on...

Roast pumpkin and chilli soup

This is a lovely warming soup that is super-quick when you've got your pumpkin prepared already.

Sauté one finely chopped onion in 1 tbsp light oil for six to eight minutes until starting to soften, add 2 finely chopped garlic cloves, 2.5cm finely chopped fresh root ginger and 2 finely chopped green chillies for two minutes. Add 800ml chicken or vegetable stock, 100g red lentils, 500g roast pumpkin and 200ml coconut milk. Bring to a boil, reduce the heat and cook gently for 15 minutes. Add a handful of coriander leaves, blend and season to taste. Serve while warm. Serves 4 for a light lunch, or 2 for a generous supper.

Pumpkin, goat's cheese, spinach and chilli rolls

These were another market stall favourite. A great vegetarian dish, meat eaters will love them too.

A fresh vegetarian roll, simply make sausage rolls as for the Lamb and Smoky Aubergine Rolls (see page 136), but fill them with goat's cheese, wilted spinach and some roast pumpkin. The filling ingredients should together weigh 600–700g, though the balance is up to you; use more cheese for a tangier roll, or more pumpkin for extra sweetness and season it well. Sprinkle with chilli flakes for some heat and roll, brush the pastry with beaten egg and bake as in the lamb recipe. Makes 4.

I first had pumpkin gnocchi many years ago when a friend's father in Naples made them for us for lunch. I was hooked immediately and they have been on the menu ever since.

Pumpkin gnocchi are a little tricky to make but, once you get the hang of them, really quick and delicious. You can have a great meal in minutes. There are a few things that you must pay attention to:

Ensure that the pumpkin is roasted until just soft, so that it retains its structure and is not too wet. If the pumpkin is really wet, allow it to drain through a sieve for a few hours. It may seem extreme but it makes a huge difference.

Work the flour in gently and quickly. If you overwork – and this can happen in just minutes – it will become gloopy and unpleasant.

Don't worry that they are difficult to shape by hand, unlike potato gnocchi. This is the way they are, they're a little messier and very light. Also don't worry about making pretty fork shapes or anything like that. They're too soft.

To make your life that bit easier, instead of rolling by hand, pipe them into the water using a disposable piping bag, cutting them with scissors into the right size as you pipe them out and letting them drop into the pan.

Pumpkin gnocchi with sage brown butter

Serves 2
500g roasted pumpkin, mashed (see page 156)
125g plain flour, plus more to dust
generous grating of nutmeg
sea salt
freshly ground black pepper
100g unsalted butter
about 12 sage leaves
Parmesan cheese, to serve (optional)

Spread the mashed pumpkin out on a tray or chopping board. Sift over the flour and add the nutmeg and some salt and pepper. Gently combine the flour with the pumpkin using a fork until there are no traces of white. The dough should be starting to come together. Place in a piping bag (see recipe introduction) or gently, with floured hands, shape them into rolls and cut gnocchi at 2.5cm sections along it.

Cook in simmering water for four to five minutes.

Meanwhile, melt the butter with the sage leaves, which will crisp as they fry. Serve the gnocchi in the melted butter with the crispy sage, shaving a little Parmesan over the top, if you like.

Home-cooked beans

Home-cooked beans are a passion of mine. Canned beans are often flaccid and depressing, swollen with salt and water they can be tasteless. Home-cooked beans are a world away. They have great texture and flavour; sure they take time, but it's not time in which you're actually doing anything, you are just leaving them to soak or simmer. Other advantages are that they are very cheap and, frozen in 300g batches, make your cooking life very convenient.

One thing to note about home-cooked beans is that they need to be relatively fresh, even when dried, or they will take forever to cook, if at all. Source them well in good shops or delis. I never cook beans with anything else, preferring to cook them separately, drain them and only then add them to what I am cooking.

Never salt beans either before or during cooking, as the salt will cause a reaction that toughens the skins. You want beautifully yielding beans, not little bullets.

Soak your beans overnight if you can, or for a minimum of six hours. Not all beans need it, but some do as they contain nasty substances that can make you ill (red kidney beans, especially, contain chemicals that will make you very ill unless soaked out). Besides, it's worth doing as all beans will cook better after soaking.

For all beans, after soaking, drain them, cover with fresh water and bring to a boil. Scoop off any scum that rises to the top, reduce the temperature and cook until the beans soften. For most this will be between 30 and 90 minutes.

All of the following recipes assume that the beans are cooked already.

This is a great hearty, gutsy dish. Home-cooked beans are in themselves quite meaty and, combined with the sausages and tomato sauce, make a great, quick dish for any time of the day. Leftovers can be served up at breakfast time, with eggs.

Haricot and sausage casserole

Serves 4
1 red onion, finely chopped
1 tbsp olive oil
300g good-quality sausages, chopped
2 garlic cloves, finely chopped
400g can chopped tomatoes
300g cooked haricot beans (homemade are best, see opposite)
250ml light chicken or vegetable stock
handful of flat leaf parsley, chopped

Sauté the onion in the oil until soft over a medium heat. Add the sausages and stir until brown on all sides. Add the garlic and cook for only a minute.

Tip in the tomatoes, beans and stock, stir, cover and cook for 15 minutes. Sprinkle with the parsley and serve warm.

This is a lovely protein-packed alternative to mash, perfect for healthier days on weeks where carbs have already featured heavily. The garlic and rosemary here lend the dish a lovely Mediterranean feel and give the otherwise dull white beans a lift.

Garlic and rosemary cannellini bean mash

Serves 1
1 garlic clove, finely chopped
2 tbsp extra virgin olive oil
1 tsp finely chopped rosemary
300g cooked cannellini beans
    (homemade are best, see page 160)
sea salt
freshly ground black pepper

Sauté the garlic in the extra virgin olive oil with the rosemary for a minute. Add all of the oil, rosemary and garlic to the beans.
    Mash lightly with a fork, keeping it quite chunky. Season with salt and pepper to taste.

Black beans are the best beans for burgers as they are the meatiest and have a dense texture which holds together quite well. Don't be put off by memories of the soggy, flaccid, depressed relatives of these that are commonly found in takeaways. These are sturdy and full-flavoured and you might find the meat eaters clamouring for them, too.

Spiced bean burgers

Makes 4
1 tsp cumin seeds
2 garlic cloves, finely chopped
1 tbsp light oil, plus more to fry
600g cooked black beans
   (homemade are best, see page 160)
½ tsp chilli flakes
50g breadcrumbs
handful of coriander leaves, chopped
1 egg, beaten

Dry-fry the cumin seeds in a small frying pan until they are aromatic and have darkened a shade. Grind to a powder in a mortar and pestle.

Fry the garlic in the oil for a minute, or until aromatic. Tip the beans into a large bowl and add the garlic and oil from the pan and all the other ingredients.

Shape the mixture into four patties and fry for about five minutes on each side over a medium heat until brown.

Sugar and Spice

When it comes to desserts – and sweet things generally – I always lean towards fruit. I love it. I like desserts that are light and, while I occasionally slip towards death by sugar and butter territory, I like to be able to get up from the dinner table afterwards and carry on with my day. I also like desserts to be fairly quick to make, although I have a few more detailed recipes here, such as Raspberry and Rose Ripple Ice Cream (see page 174).

Childhood memories of blackberries, rhubarb, gooseberries and apples permeate my sweet consciousness, as does my obsession with lemon curd which has somewhat evolved. I've always adored meringue pies and think they're terribly underrated, while my passion for the simple éclair knows no bounds. I first tried to make choux pastry when I was too young to be wielding a hot pan, such was my desperation to have one. Living in the countryside nowhere near a shop forces resourcefulness and creativity!

My mother always endeavoured to get me to drink milk or eat any dairy as a child, but outside of desserts and yogurts I wasn't at all interested. Then I discovered gooseberry and rhubarb fools made with yogurt and cream and I was sold. It's not quite healthy, but the compromise was enough for my mother to concede and allow my indulgence. I was a tiny thing then and my body could take the calorie load. I am not so fortunate now, but I do indulge occasionally. You just have to, don't you?

Quinces are fantastic, aromatic with delicate perfume. They're wonderful in season and also available jarred all year round. (If you use jarred, omit the boiling stage here.)

There are dedicated tarte Tatin pans, and it is best to use one, but if you don't have one, use a 20cm ovenproof frying pan. I use shop-bought puff pastry, as the all-butter stuff is really good and there's no need to put yourself through the trauma of making it.

Rosehips in season are bountiful but, if they are out of season, you can source dried hips easily online from beer brewing websites. They are packed with Vitamin C, a bonus!

If you can't face making sorbet, this is delicious with vanilla crème fraîche, too. Just scrape the seeds from half a vanilla pod into a pot of crème fraîche and stir.

Quince tarte Tatin with rosehip sorbet

Serves 4

For the rosehip sorbet
150g dried rosehips, crushed
   (or double that amount, fresh)
225g caster sugar
juice of 1 unwaxed lemon

For the tarte Tatin
4 quinces
150g caster sugar
500g all-butter puff pastry
100g unsalted butter

Bring the rosehips and sugar to a boil with 850ml water. When the sugar dissolves, take from the heat and allow to cool. Strain and add the lemon when cold. For best results, churn in an ice cream maker. If you don't have one, put in the freezer in a covered container. After an hour, whisk. Repeat every 30 minutes. It should be ready after two hours.

Preheat the oven to 190°C/375°F/gas mark 5. Peel the quinces and cut into 1cm wedges. I take the seeds out but, if you prefer the quinces to be pink, leave them in until cooked. Place in a saucepan, cover with water and add 50g of the sugar. Bring to a boil and cook until tender (about 20 minutes). Drain. Remove the seeds and cores, if you left them in.

Roll the pastry to 5mm thick and large enough to cover your pan. Prick with a fork all over and keep in the fridge until you need it.

Caramelise the butter and remaining sugar in a saucepan by melting gently until golden brown. Be careful not to burn it. Arrange the quinces in the pan to cover the base, then pour the caramel over. Cook for 15 minutes to allow to caramelise, then cover with the pastry. Cook for 30 minutes, until golden and crisp. Serve warm with the sorbet.

Tip: if you leave the seeds in the quinces while boiling, they go a little pink. Leave them out, they stay yellow! Up to you, whichever you prefer.

✦ PASSION ✦

Blackberry and crème fraîche filo tart

This is one of the desserts from my market stall, made when blackberries were in season. It's very simple, layers of crispy filo with crème fraîche, berries, mint and honey between. Baked until crisp, it's a terrific late summer dessert. It's also very quick with shop-bought filo. There is really no need to make filo pastry at home.

Serves 4–6
125g unsalted butter, melted, plus more for the tin
500g crème fraîche
400g blackberries
50ml honey
about 12 mint leaves, shredded
250g pack filo pastry

Butter a 20cm square ovenproof dish, and preheat the oven to 180°C/350°F/gas mark 4.

Combine the crème fraîche, blackberries, honey and mint. Mix gently; you don't want to crush the blackberries too much.

Divide the filo sheets into four groups. Place the first lot on the bottom of the dish, brushing each layer generously with melted butter.

Put one-third of the crème fraîche and blackberry mix on top. Cover with the next layer of filo and repeat until there are four layers of filo and three of filling, ensuring each filo sheet is brushed with butter.

Bake for 15–20 minutes until the filo is crisp. Eat warm or cold.

Another market favourite, I made these cute little tarts in muffin tins. The recipe is relatively quick as it uses shop-bought filo and is really fresh and delicious. This tart is especially good with Homemade Ricotta (see page 70) that has been drained so it is quite firm. If you are using shop-bought ricotta, drain it, as it can be a bit too wet.

Raspberry and ricotta tarts

Serves 6
300ml ricotta (homemade is best, see page 70)
1 egg
75ml double cream
50g golden caster sugar
12 mint leaves, finely chopped
250g filo pastry
150g unsalted butter, melted
300g raspberries

Drain the ricotta in a sieve or a bundle of muslin until it has lost most of its moisture. Preheat the oven to 180°C/350°F/gas mark 4.

Combine the ricotta with the egg, cream and sugar and whip with a mixer or electric whisk until smooth. Add the mint leaves and stir through until evenly distributed.

Butter a six-cup muffin tray. Cut the filo into 15cm squares and put four layers in each cup, buttering each as you go. Arrange the layers so that you get lots of edges pointing out at the top.

Divide the ricotta mixture between the tartlets and bake for 15–20 minutes, until the pastry is a crisp brown.

Allow to cool slightly, then arrange the raspberries on top. Serve cool.

Candying fruit is an ancient way of preserving it, driving out the water and replacing it with sugars makes it last so much longer. Candied orange zests dipped in chocolate are an old French sweet that still taste great today. Make a large batch of them and store in an airtight jar for emergencies.

Orangettes

Makes 30–35
2 large oranges
150g sugar
100g best dark chocolate

Peel the oranges from top to bottom, ensuring the zest comes off in strips. Scrape off and discard any white pith that clings to the zest. Cut the zest into equal widths of about 5mm.

Bring a saucepan of water to a boil, tip in the orange zest strips and boil for a few minutes to remove any bitterness. Drain.

Make a stock syrup by heating the sugar and 150ml water until the sugar is dissolved. Bring to a boil. Add the zest strips, bring to a boil again, reduce the heat, cover and simmer for an hour or so, taking care to ensure that the zest strips are covered with syrup at all times. Drain and allow to cool.

Melt the chocolate in a heatproof bowl over gently simmering water, making sure the bowl does not touch the water. Dip in the candied strips so that half of each is covered in chocolate. Place on a wire rack to drain, with a piece of greaseproof paper underneath to catch the drips.

Allow to cool and they are ready to serve. Perfect with tea or coffee, or as a sneaky snack.

This really simple and delicious recipe is deliberately dairy free, so it's perfect for those that are lactose intolerant or dairy allergic. It's also relatively guilt free. Good chocolate is actually quite good for you, as long as you are not eating it by the truckload.

I learned the mousse recipe in school and made it obsessively when younger. There are raw eggs here but don't be afraid of that, source them well and all is good. This is the way chocolate mousse was always made. As there are only two ingredients in it, make sure you use really good chocolate and really good eggs, you will taste the quality.

The honeycomb recipe is very easy but takes a little care. Do invest in a sugar or jam thermometer and watch it. If it looks like it is getting too dark, it is burning, so take it off the heat. Use a high-sided pan as, when you add the bicarb, the sugar will go crazy and rise to several times its size. This is also the phase where you are most likely to burn yourself, so do take care. Those warnings aside it's a really fun thing to make, so do try it and enjoy it. Any leftovers make terrific homemade sweets, covered in dark chocolate.

Chocolate mousse with honeycomb

Serves 6

For the mousse
180g best dark chocolate
6 eggs, separated

For the honeycomb
light oil, for the tin
300g white sugar (caster or granulated)
200g golden syrup
1 tbsp cider or white wine vinegar
2 heaped tsp bicarbonate of soda

First make your honeycomb. Prepare a tin or heatproof dish by lining with lightly oiled baking parchment. Heat the sugar, syrup, 100ml water and vinegar until it turns amber and reaches 150°C (the 'hard crack' stage). Add the bicarb and stir well, then pour into your lined tin. Leave to cool to room temperature. If you want it in ordered shapes, cut with an oiled knife when it's nearly at room temperature. I like it to look a little rough and tumble, so cut it when it's cool.

For the mousse, break the chocolate into squares and melt gently in a double boiler, or in a saucepan over another saucepan of simmering water, until melted. Meanwhile, whisk the egg whites until stiff.

Once the chocolate is melted, remove from the heat and whisk in the egg yolks (they will cook if you keep them on the heat; you don't want scrambled egg in your mousse). When combined, gently add the egg whites, taking care not to knock out any of the air you have whisked in. Don't worry too much if it doesn't look very mousse like at this stage, it will be lovely when it's set. Pour into your serving glasses and leave in the fridge for two hours. Serve with honeycomb shards on top.

✦ PASSION ✦

Orange and cardamom jelly with clotted cream

Ice cream and jelly was a favourite childhood dessert and I still love to have it although now I eat more grown-up versions. I do love jelly on its own, especially with more adult flavours such as spices involved, but I love to serve this one with clotted cream, that wonderful rich preserved cream from Cornwall. Orange and cardamom is a very festive ice cream, but works well all year round. Again, it's a ridiculously easy dessert.

Serves 6
8 cardamom pods
1 litre fresh orange juice (about 10 oranges, depending on size)
finely grated zest and juice of 2 unwaxed lemons
50g golden caster sugar
8 gelatine sheets
clotted cream, to serve

Bruise the cardamom pods with the back of a knife and add to the citrus juices, lemon zest and sugar in a saucepan. Bring just to a boil, then take off the heat. Allow to sit for 15 minutes to let the cardamom infuse.

Meanwhile, cover the gelatine with cold water.

After 15 minutes, while the juice is still warm, strain it through a sieve. Squeeze the gelatine leaves to get rid of excess water and add to the warmed, sieved juice. Stir to dissolve the gelatine.

Pour the juice into six individual glasses, leaving room on top for a spoon of clotted cream. Leave to chill and set in the fridge for four to six hours. Serve cold with the clotted cream on top.

Crème brûlée is a relatively simple and impressive dessert. It's just a baked custard with a caramelised sugar crust on top. Simple! It's very like making the custard for an ice cream (see overleaf) so once you've conquered one, be sure to try the other. I make homemade pistachio nut butter to give this a lovely twist. Make extra nut butter and save it in the fridge to spread on toast for very quick breakfasts.

You will need to make these in advance to allow them to set. For a little extra drama, caramelise the sugar on top with a cook's blow torch.

Pistachio crème brûlée

Serves 4
For the brûlées
500ml double cream
75g caster sugar, plus about 8 tsp for the topping
1 tsp vanilla extract
4 large egg yolks

For the pistachio nut butter
100g shelled unsalted pistachio nuts
1 tsp sea salt
1 tbsp groundnut oil

Preheat the oven to 150°C/300°F/gas mark 2.

Heat the cream and sugar over a medium heat until just before a boil. Add the vanilla and take from the heat. Leave to cool for 10 minutes.

Make your nut butter by blending the pistachio nuts with the salt, adding as much of the oil as you need to get a firm butter. Don't purée completely, it's best to leave some chunks in.

In a bowl, beat the egg yolks until frothy. Slowly add the cooled cream mixture, whisking as you do. It's important that you add it slowly so it doesn't cook the eggs. Strain the mixture to remove any stringy bits which may have formed.

Pour into four ramekins and place in a deep roasting tin. Stir 1 tbsp of the nut butter into each to make a ripple effect. Pour hot water from a boiled kettle into the tin so that it comes halfway up each ramekin. Bake for half an hour, or until the brûlées are set but have a slight wobble.

Allow to cool and chill in the fridge for at least two hours, or overnight.

When ready to serve, sprinkle about 2 tsp sugar on top of each and put under the grill until caramelised, or torch with a cook's blow torch.

My childhood memories of ice cream are fierce. My grandfather always had a supply in his freezer and when we were good we were allowed a slice between wafers. Once, when tiny, I refused to eat my lunch of a huge and intimidating pile of mash with lots of peas which I loathed. My grandmother wouldn't cave and nor would I. So I sat for what seemed like an eternity watching my cousins playing out the window. Eventually, my grandfather whisked me out, gave me some ice cream and put me out in the back garden where my grandmother wouldn't see me eat the forbidden treat.

My favourite, then and now, was raspberry ripple. I love to add rose now. Rose and raspberries are terrific together and make the ice cream that little bit more elegant.

Homemade ice cream is a little finicky but worth the trouble, especially for creating unusual flavours that you can't buy. It will also taste better (of course!). You can make it by hand by taking it out of the freezer every 30 minutes or so and whisking, but I say an ice cream machine is a worthwhile and great-value investment.

Raspberry and rose ripple ice cream

Makes about 1.5 litres
For the ice cream
1 vanilla pod
600ml double cream
600ml full-fat milk
200g golden caster sugar
6 large egg yolks

For the raspberry and rose ripple
400g raspberries
50g golden caster sugar
2 tbsp rose water

Halve the vanilla pod and scrape the seeds into the cream and milk in a saucepan. Add the pod and sugar and bring to a gentle simmer. When the sugar has dissolved, take it from the heat and remove the vanilla pod (the seeds will remain). Whisk the egg yolks until they thicken. Slowly add the cream, initially in only a trickle so as not to scramble the yolks.

Now, put the custard into a clean pan over a very low heat, stirring so it doesn't burn. After 15 minutes it should coat the back of a spoon. Put in a bowl and cover. Allow to cool, stirring to prevent a skin forming.

Once it has cooled, churn in an ice cream machine. Meanwhile, bring the raspberries, 50ml water and the sugar to a boil and cook until it reduces to a sticky sauce; it will take about five minutes. Then add your rose water. Intensify the flavour by reducing a little further and your ripple is done. If you don't like seeds, sieve it, but I like to keep them in.

Add some of the churned ice cream to a freezer container, then some of the ripple, then repeat until it's all in there. Use a palette knife to ripple it through. Freeze, or serve immediately.

✦ PASSION ✦

Chilli chocolate truffles

Chocolate truffles are gorgeous, a perfect petit four at the end of a meal. Sinfully rich and ridiculously easy, I find that a gentle chilli heat raises the bar. Use the best chocolate you can get as this is the primary flavour. Bad chocolate = bad truffles. I add a little salt as it goes so well with the chocolate. People won't even know that it is in there, it is very subtle.

Makes about 20
250ml double cream
pinch of sea salt
50g unsalted butter
1 red chilli, halved and deseeded
250g dark chocolate (at least 70% cocoa solids), grated or finely chopped
50g cocoa powder, sifted

In a saucepan, heat the cream, salt and butter gently with the chilli, until it starts to move. Don't boil it.

Take it from the heat, remove the chilli and add the chocolate, stirring to melt. Allow it to cool, then to solidify in the fridge. Overnight is easiest, but for at least four hours.

Scoop out a teaspoonful at a time and roll gently in the cocoa powder.
They are ready to eat.

I first had cakes like these in one of my favourite ice cream shops in London, Gelupo. As I took a bite I thought, WOW, I've got to try and make these at home. So I did. They contain olive oil in place of butter and make a really good snack with a cup of tea or coffee. These are gorgeous with blood oranges in season, but normal oranges are fine.

Little polenta, almond and blood orange cakes

Makes about 12, depending on the size of your moulds
2 tbsp honey
2 whole blood oranges, peeled, in 1cm dice
150g plain flour, plus more for the tin
1 tbsp baking powder
pinch of sea salt
225g polenta
100g ground almonds
75g golden caster sugar
3 eggs, separated
juice from 4 blood oranges and finely grated zest of 1
225ml olive oil, plus more for the tin
icing sugar, to dust (optional)

Preheat the oven to 180°C/350°F/gas mark 4. Combine the honey with the diced oranges and leave to the side while you prepare and bake the cakes. This will create a lovely syrup for the top.

Sift the flour, baking powder and salt into a mixing bowl and stir in the polenta, almonds and sugar.

Whisk together the egg yolks, orange juice, zest and oil and stir through the flour mixture gently, keeping the air that you have sifted in.

Whisk the egg whites until fluffy as you would for meringue (this makes the cakes lovely and light). Fold gently through the other ingredients. Bake in a lightly oiled and floured bun tray for 40 minutes, until they spring back to the touch.

Remove and cool on a wire rack. Serve with the blood oranges and honey poured over the top. Dust with icing sugar, if you like.

✦ PASSION ✦

Elderflower and gooseberry fool

Gooseberries are a wonderful fruit, I think I loved them even more as I was the only child in the house that liked them so I had them all to myself. My aunt grew them in her fruit patch and I would pick them, wondering if they would be too sour, or gone too far and then too sweet and lacking in flavour. I was never sure and, when I hit one that was right, I would devour more.

The tart gooseberries work very well with cream in a gooseberry fool; let's face it, what doesn't? Elderflower is a perfect match for it, too. I make my fool simply with whipped cream for a quick and simple summer dessert. If you want to make it more of a breakfast dish, mix the gooseberries with Greek yogurt instead of cream, or use half and half for a more health-conscious dessert.

Serves 4
400g gooseberries, topped and tailed
100ml elderflower cordial
about 50g caster sugar (depends on how tart
your gooseberries are, so taste to check)
500ml double cream, lightly whipped

Cook the gooseberries with the elderflower cordial and sugar until soft and mushy. Taste to ensure it is sweet enough, though bear in mind that the taste will be muted a bit by the cream.

Let the gooseberries cool and stir gently through the cream to create a marbled effect. Spoon into individual glasses and serve chilled.

✦ PASSION ✦

Two curds, but I can't help it. It's important to make curd in a double boiler, or improvise one with a saucepan sitting over another filled with simmering water. This allows the curd to cook in a gentler fashion and ensures, with regular stirring, that the eggs don't turn into omelette. Both these curds will keep for a couple of weeks in the fridge.

Curd is wonderful on sourdough toast. It also makes a terrific fruit fool; stirred into cream cheese it is a cheesecake topping; or with broken meringues, cream and blueberries, a non-traditional Eton mess.

Rhubarb and blood orange curd

Makes 2 small jars
200g rhubarb, trimmed and chopped
50g unsalted butter, plus a few knobs
50g caster sugar
finely grated zest of 1 blood orange and juice of 2
2 whole eggs, plus 2 egg yolks

Preheat the oven to 150°C/300°F/gas mark 2. Roast the rhubarb for 15 minutes until tender. Drain in a sieve. Meanwhile, melt the butter and sugar in a double boiler. Add the zest, juice, eggs and yolks and cook gently, stirring. When it coats the back of a spoon, take it from the heat. Stir through the rhubarb. Store in a covered bowl or jars.

Passion fruit and lime curd

Makes 2 small jars
75g unsalted butter
75g caster sugar
3 passion fruits, seeds and pulp scraped out
finely grated zest and juice of 1 lime
2 whole eggs, plus 2 egg yolks

Melt the butter and sugar in a double boiler. Add the passion fruit seeds and pulp, zest, juice, eggs and yolks. Cook gently, stirring, until the curd coats the back of a spoon. It will thicken as it cools. Store in a covered bowl or jars.

I love meringue pie, it's utterly comforting, nostalgic and just beautiful to eat. It's especially nice in January, after an endless parade of green and brown food, when the gorgeous Yorkshire forced rhubarb and bright blood oranges arrive. If you can't get blood oranges, feel free to substitute normal oranges.

Lots of meringue pie recipes call for cornflour to thicken the curd, but I prefer not to use it here. Some time in the fridge will allow it all to set. The results are a little sloppier than the traditional version perhaps, but the flavour is terrific.

Rhubarb and blood orange meringue pie

Makes a 25cm tart
For the sweet shortcrust pastry
75g unsalted butter, chilled and diced
150g plain flour, sifted, plus more to dust
25g icing sugar, sifted
1 egg yolk, lightly beaten with the same amount of water

For the filling
1 x quantity Rhubarb and Blood Orange Curd (see page 179)

For the meringue
3 egg whites
50g icing sugar, sifted
25g cornflour

To make the pastry, add the butter to the flour and icing sugar and rub it in with your fingertips until it looks like crumbs. Add the egg to bring together, mould into a ball, wrap in cling film and chill for an hour.

Preheat the oven to 180°C/350°F/gas mark 4. Roll the pastry out until big enough to line a 25cm pie dish. Line with baking parchment, fill with baking beans, and blind bake for 20–25 minutes. Increase the oven temperature to 200°C/400°F/gas mark 6. Pour the curd into the shell.

Whisk the egg whites until starting to form stiff peaks, add half the sugar, whisk again, then sift in the cornflour and gently fold in with the remaining sugar. Spoon the meringue on top of the curd, trying to create lots of little peaks that will brown and ensuring it touches the pastry edge. Bake for five minutes or so, until starting to brown.

Allow the tart to cool and the curd to set for a couple of hours in the fridge. Serve cold. Try not to eat it all in one sitting, as I have done!

I remember baking an apple in school and being amazed at the results. I immediately started to calculate how many I could make from the apple tree down the road. A lot! I tired of it pretty quickly as I overindulged, but I do love making this simple, flavourful and healthy dessert as an adult.

Our school recipe had lots of dried fruit. I prefer to keep these simple, adding cinnamon, sugar and butter to the inside. I use cooking apples: Bramleys are great.

Baked apple

Serves 4
4 Bramley apples
4 tsp calvados
4 tsp brown sugar
1 tsp ground cinnamon
4 tsp unsalted butter, plus more for the tray

Preheat the oven to 180°C/350°F/gas mark 4.

Core the apple and, halfway down each, cut a fine line across its equator through the skin to the flesh. This will ensure that the apple won't burst. A handy tip!

Put 1 tsp of calvados in each apple followed by 1 tsp sugar and a pinch of cinnamon. Finish with 1 tsp butter.

Put the apples in a buttered baking tray and pour some water in, just enough to cover the tray. Bake for 45–50 minutes until the apples are soft. Serve hot as they are, or with some Greek yogurt on top.

Baked cheesecake brings back memories of a birthday in Paris. We took the Eurostar at stupid o'clock and spent the night. After spending an enthusiastic day walking and walking, and eating and eating, I could hardly move by sunset. My birthday meal was predominantly a battle with my eyelids, which were determined to close.

The next day, a wander around the Marais revealed the wonder of baked ricotta cheesecake in an Orthodox Jewish bakery. I had a slice there and took another for the Eurostar journey home. It has been a favourite ever since. I like to make it slightly differently with lemon and blueberry to give it a bit of a spritz.

Lemon and blueberry ricotta cheesecake

Serves 6
500g ricotta (homemade is best, see page 70)
4 eggs
180g caster sugar
50g plain flour, sifted
juice of 2 unwaxed lemons
100g blueberries
unsalted butter, for the tin

Preheat the oven to 150°C/300°F/gas mark 2.

Whisk the ricotta, eggs and sugar until frothy. Add the flour and lemon juice and whisk until smooth. Stir in the blueberries gently.

Butter a 20cm cake tin and pour in the batter. Bake for 30 minutes. Check that the cake is set in the centre – it should be – but if it's not give it a few more minutes.

Allow to cool and served sliced.

This will accentuate any table and refresh on a hot summer's day. The rose water is subtle, you want a gentle flavour not the sensation of drinking perfume.

Cucumber and rose water

Serves 4
1 cucumber, cut into long strips with a vegetable peeler
petals from 1 organic rose
1 tbsp rose water

Combine all the ingredients in a glass jug – you will want to show off
this pretty drink – with 1 litre of water and lots of ice. Serve immediately.

Really refreshing; lovely on a sunny afternoon, with a spicy Prawn Curry (see page 41).

Mango and mint lassi

Serves 4
2 mangos
600ml yogurt (homemade is best, see page 12)
400ml full-fat milk
handful of fresh mint leaves, shredded

Purée the mangos, yogurt and milk. Add the mint and stir through.
Refrigerate until you want to serve it.

Chilli may seem odd in a drink but mild chilli has a gentle kick which, against ice, gives a lovely hot-cold sensation. Lemon grass gives aroma and sweet mandarin loves it all.

Mandarin, chilli and lemon grass juice

Serves 4
750g mandarins, juiced
1 lemon grass stalk, trimmed and finely chopped
½ mild red chilli, deseeded and finely chopped

Blend all the ingredients until you can no longer see any chunks of
lemon grass and only flecks of chilli remain. Serve with lots of ice.

Rosehip and lemon martini

Makes 1
50ml gin (I like Hendricks as it has rose notes which work well here)
25ml vermouth
1 tsp rosehip syrup
squeeze of unwaxed lemon, plus a lemon twist to serve

The glamorous bit! Add all the liquids to a cocktail shaker (or jam jar if you're stuck) with ice, and strain to serve with your dapper lemon twist.

Rhubarb and rose bellini

Makes 5
350g rhubarb, chopped
2 tbsp caster sugar (unnecessary for forced rhubarb)
up to 2 tbsp rose water
1 bottle of prosecco, chilled

Preheat the oven to 180°C/350°F/gas mark 4. Roast the rhubarb for 15 minutes until soft. Stir in the sugar to dissolve, if needed, and cool.

Add the rose water in teaspoons and check the flavour. Early season, pink, sweet (particularly forced) rhubarb won't need much; midsummer greener rhubarb – extraordinarily tart at times – may need more.

Put 2 tsp of this compote into five champagne flutes. Top up with chilled prosecco, stir and serve immediately.

Elderflower bellini

Makes 5
For the bellini
1 bottle prosecco, chilled

For the elderflower cordial
100g caster sugar
12 heads of elderflowers
1 unwaxed lemon, cut in half

Dissolve the sugar in 750ml water. Cool. Add the elderflowers. Squeeze in the lemon and add its shell. Refrigerate to infuse for a couple of days. Strain and refrigerate.

To make the bellini, add 1 tsp of cordial to each flute of prosecco. Stir and check the flavour, adding more if needed. Serve immediately.

Mulled wine

Serves 8–10

3 clementines, halved

2 bottles red wine (Montepulciano d'Abruzzo works really well)

250ml port

2 cinnamon sticks

2 bay leaves

75g brown sugar

12 cloves

1 nutmeg

Gently squeeze the clementines into a pot containing the wine, port, cinnamon, bay leaves and sugar. Stud the clementine shells with the cloves and add them. Grate in one-third of the nutmeg. Bring to just before a boil, ensuring the sugar is dissolved. Check the sweetness. Allow to cool a little and serve after 10–15 minutes.

Spiced cider

Serves 6

1 litre good cider

150ml cider brandy

2 cinnamon sticks

75g caster sugar (this assumes a sour cider)

6 allspice berries

1 nutmeg

1 firm apple, cored and cut into thick slices

12 cloves

Put the cider and brandy in a pot with the cinnamon and sugar. Bash the allspice and add. Grate in one-third of the nutmeg. Stud the apple slices with cloves and drop them in. Gently bring to just above a boil and check the sweetness. Allow to cool slightly and serve after 10 minutes.

Irish hot port

Serves 1

1 tsp brown sugar

70ml port

1 unwaxed lemon slice, studded with 4 cloves

Dissolve the sugar in 70ml just-boiled hot water and add the port. Lightly squeeze in the lemon slice and add the slice. Serve immediately.

Acknowledgements

This book would never have happened if people hadn't read my blog, so to all my readers, thank you!

Thanks, in particular, to my family for their unending support, especially my mother for always encouraging me to follow whatever it is that I want to do, and for buying me all of those cookery magazines when I was younger!

To Art for his unfailing faith in what I do, his honest criticism and his generous palate.

To my agent Clare for believing in what I wanted to do and helping me choose the best publisher for me, Quadrille.

To Ben, my market manager, for his incredible support and encouragement.

To Quadrille for publishing me, for being fantastically supportive, for letting me determine how this should go, particularly Anne, Mark, Clare and Nikki.

To my editor Lucy for her patience, support and wisdom.

To my wonderful photographer Georgia Glynn Smith for being brilliant and encouraging, and for interpreting my style perfectly for this book.

Thank you, too, for buying this book.